BREAKING THE POWER

The Workbook

BREAKING THE POWER

The Workbook
by
Liberty Savard

Bridge-Logos *Publishers*

Gainesville, Florida 32614 USA

Breaking the Power Workbook
by Liberty Savard

Copyright © 2000 by Liberty Savard
International Standard Book Number: 0-88270-786-8
All information in this workbook is based upon the book, *Breaking the Power*, written by Rev. Liberty S. Savard (Bridge-Logos Publishers, 1997). No portion of this material may be reproduced without the written permission of the author of *Breaking the Power*.
Reprint 2001

Published by:
Bridge-Logos *Publishers*
Gainesville, FL 32614
http://www.bridgelogos.com

Acknowledgments

Special thanks to Pastor Dan Cook for his help in finalizing this workbook.

The Keys of the Kingdom Trilogy
by Liberty Savard:

• *Shattering Your Strongholds*

• *Breaking the Power*

• *Producing the Promise*

Also available:

• *Shattering Your Strongholds Workbook*

For further information on speaking engagements, seminars, current U.S. itinerary, teaching tapes, workbooks, television programs, and free teaching newsletters published quarterly, please contact:

Liberty Savard Ministries, Inc.
(a non-profit organization)
P.O. Box 41260
Sacramento, CA 95841-0260

Office phone: 916-721-7770
Facsimile: 916-721-8889

E-mail: liberty@libertysavard.com
Web site: http://www.libertysavard.com

Contents

Introduction

So you are now ready to Break the Power of your soul's unmet needs, unhealed hurts, and unresolved issues. Good for you! You are moving into the second level of revelation of the most effective use of the keys of the Kingdom of binding and loosing in principles of prayer.

With the book ***Breaking the Power***, this study guide will take you deeper into understanding the unsurrendered soul's hidden agendas and motives, learning how it uses old memories and fears to control your life. Whether you work through the workbook by yourself in a self-study program, or you are part of a study group, you will learn new ways of praying that will enable you to cooperate with God in the renewing of your mind, the healing of your emotions, and the surrendering of your will.

As His child, you can cooperate with or rebel against this process.
You can continue always **being worked on by God**,
or you can choose to pick up the keys Christ has given to you
and **begin to work with God**.
This should not be a hard choice to make.

You will be able to finally open up the three main sources of your inner pain so God can fix what most needs fixing. You will be able to see how He really does know what needs fixing first, and you will begin to relax about letting Him shake out the details, the order, and the time frame of His plan of restoration for your life. Three things that have plagued you for years will be opened up to His great grace and mercy and love—for you hold the keys to breaking the chains of the prison doors created by these <u>three sources of all your struggles</u>:

Your unmet needs—birthed in your soul when something positive that should have happened in your life **didn't happen**.

Your unhealed hurts—birthed in your soul when something negative that should not have happened in your life **did happen**.

Your unresolved issues—birthed in your soul by the ensuing anger and confusion about **why**.

The questions are designed to focus your thoughts on points of understanding that could be overlooked while reading the book. Try to relate each question to your own life first, then to the lives of others.

For example, question 27 of chapter 2 asks: What does our soul do to keep us from having true knowledge of God?

The answer is found at the top of page 22 in the **Breaking the Power** book (sentence actually starts on bottom of 21): The soul thinks its job description is to throw up arguments, reasonings, and logic—strongholds—between itself and a knowledge of God.

The second part of the same question asks you to focus on your own relationship with God and to try to name an area where you are aware that your soul has kept you from a full surrender. Attempt to consider each question from such a personal point of view.

Do not rush through the following questions. The object of this workbook is not to just fill in the blanks—the object is to recognize how your soul has been pursuing its own self-protective agendas even after you became born again as a Christian. Jesus Christ became the link or the bridge between your regenerated spirit and the Spirit of your Creator. Your unsurrendered soul began running, ducking, and dodging the ramifications of that blood-bought bridge to God almost immediately.

There are additional resources available to further enhance your study of **Breaking the Power**:

1. **Breaking the Power** Video Seminar. Ten 77-minute video tapes of chapter-by-chapter teaching, with each chapter's teaching being broken into three 24 ½ minute segments which are perfect for 30 consecutive discussion groups or 30 consecutive Sunday school classes. Each chapter's video cassette will enhance your chapter studies, although the video teachings do not follow the exact order of questions in the workbook.
2. **Breaking the Power** Video Seminar Soundtracks on audio cassettes.
3. **Breaking the Power** Book on Tape as read word for word by author.
4. **Unsurrendered Soul Chart** (graphics and prayer) mentioned in the book.

For further information on these resources and more, access our website at http://www.libertysavard.com, or call our ministry offices at (916) 721-7770, or fax us at (916) 721-8889, or mail us at P.O. Box 41260, Sacramento, CA 95841.

<u>**You can**</u> overcome wrong behaviors.
<u>**You can**</u> receive God's unconditional love.
<u>**You can**</u> come completely out of the torment of fear and shame.
Are you ready?

The Bridge

1. What do we know about Jesus' actions when He was dealing with evil spirits?

_____

_____

_____

_____

2. In the Gospels, we do not find any record of Jesus binding what?

_____

Nor do we find any record of Jesus using **what two acts of loosing** that many Christians are using today?

_____

_____

3. What did the author believe the enemy was initially doing to keep her from dealing with her unsurrendered soul?

_____

_____

_____

4. What did the author say the enemy's deception kept her from doing?

_____

_____

5. Satan is not _____. He is _____.

6. What is one major reason so many in the Church have not used the keys of the Kingdom effectively to walk in more spiritual victory?

_____

7. What wrong pattern of thinking are we liable to place intense faith in, in spite of ourselves?

_____

8. What is the REAL conflict we need to understand so we can stop wasting time?

_____

_____

9. What is the author referring to as "so-called spiritual victories"?

_____

_____

10. What is our real problem?_____Who is our
false surrogate problem? _____

11. What does the author say the entire book can help you recognize?

_____

_____

Loosing Attitudes of the Soul Instead of Loosing Spirits

12. What examples are given of attitudes of an unsurrendered soul within a Christian?

_____

_____

_____

13. Casting out demons and spirits never bring permanent relief when:

_____

_____

14. Deliverance does nothing to bring:

_____

You can't be delivered from what?

_____

15. When can evil spirits become involved in a person's life?

_____

_____

16. What does this cause to happen?

_____

17. What must be done to close the open doors of access in the unsurrendered soul to prevent the return of spiritual harassment?

_____

_____

18. Where must the path to permanent freedom and wholeness be taken?

_____

_____

What has happened to many who have not known this?

_____

_____

Binding and Loosing Reviewed

19. The Hebrew and Greek words for "bind" and "binding" mean some very positive things such as:

_____

_____

_____

20. The Greek word for "loose," *luo*, along with **rhegnumi** and **agnumi** mean:

_____

_____

_____

_____

_____

21. Loose is a powerful word that can be used in prayer to accomplish what three things?

_____

_____

_____

_____

Jesus Keeps It Simple

22. What have our minds, wills, and emotions faithfully squirreled away?

_____

_____

23. These sources cause what three things in our lives?

_____

24. Why do past traumas hurt us today?

_____

_____

25. What is the source of the remaining power our past traumas has over us?

_____

26. Why is it dangerous to give in to the unsurrendered soul's insistence that it must be the controlling factor in the healing of our memories?

_____

_____

27. What is the unsurrendered soul's control in our lives based upon?

_____

_____

28. Christians who don't know how to tear down their souls' strongholds prevent God from doing what?

_____

_____

29. Jesus never wanted Christians to be dependent upon anything other than:

_____

_____

30. Jesus never wanted His lambs dependent on counselors, programs, or groups. However, such entities may:

_____

_____

31. What can the keys of the Kingdom dismantle?

_____

_____

_____

32. This dismantling can be accomplished how?

_____

_____

_____

33. God will not do what to heal us?

_____

Why not?

_____

_____

Cooperating with Your Own Healing and Deliverance

34. What must we know how to do in order to stop guarding our areas of _____ so Jesus can heal us?

_____

_____

35. Regardless of your soul's many efforts, analyzing and working through _____

will not _____ you.

36. Jesus always seeks permission to _____ _____ the most _____, _____ _____ of our pain without _____ us.

37. Our wills' soulish defense systems, built of strongholds, do what?

_____

_____

38. What six things make up our personal inner strongholds?

_____

_____

39. What do wrong beliefs help us deny?

_____

_____

_____

40. What are our strongholds of human reasoning and self justification trying to get us to believe?

_____

_____

_____

_____

41. When can God move our souls into perfect alignment with our bodies and our spirits?

_____

_____

_____

42. What is the definition of "synergy" the author paraphrases from *Webster's Dictionary*?

_____

_____

_____

In other words . . . the sum total of the efforts of our bodies, souls, and spirits working together in perfect synergy could be _____, _____, or maybe even _____ effects!

43. What is the Greek meaning of the word "suffering" in Romans 8:17?

_____

_____

_____

44. What is this verse actually saying then?

_____

_____

_____

More Training-Wheel Prayers

45. The binding and loosing "training-wheel prayers" are designed to help everyone _____

_____

_____

46. Since these prayers are deliberately written to be thought provoking, the author encourages you to do what three things?

_____

_____

_____

_____

_____

47. Is it all right to adjust pronouns from personal to names of others in these prayers?

_____

48. What will cause the most struggling as you pray these principles for yourself and others?

_____

When you feel in conflict with the concepts of praying this way, bind your will to the will of God and your mind to the mind of Christ, loose the control from your soul and all hindrances and devices of the enemy from your life which are trying to confuse and unsettle you.

The Bridge - Review

The most significant truths I found in this chapter are:

1. _____
_____
_____

2. _____
_____
_____

3. _____
_____
_____

4. _____
_____
_____

I applied these truths to my life as follows:

1. _____
_____
_____

2. _____
_____
_____

3. _____
_____
_____

4. _____
_____
_____

The Bridge - "Journey" Journal

Date: **Questions I have:**

Date: **Special insights I believe I have learned:**

Date: **Breakthroughs I have experienced:**

The Bridge - Prayer Journal

Date: **Prayer:**

Date: **Updates and special encouragements I've received from the Lord:**

Date: **Answers to prayers:**

1
Don't Look Back for Your Destiny

God is in control of our destiny and nothing and no one in the world can alter His purposes for it. We_____ affect the amount of time we will have to actually walk in the fullness of _____ _____ while still on earth. _____ of how much time we waste here by struggling with ourselves and our issues, this author believes we will step into the plans God has always had for us—even if it is only for a _____ _____ of _____.

1. What is the outcome of the choices we make? (circle one)
   a) the length of the journey
   b) the destination

2. We are: (circle one)
   a) Human beings having a spiritual experience on earth
   b) Spiritual beings for all time and eternity having a human experience on earth

Sowing and Reaping

3. As believers, our pasts, our presents, and our futures, are about what?

_____

4. Galatians 6:7 (AMP) tells us: _____

_____

5. If we did not sow the seeds of abuse and lack into our own lives in earlier years . . .
(complete the sentence)

_____

6. How does the author describe the "imperfect people" we've all had in our pasts?

_____

_____

_____

7. We _____ _____ have to _____
_____ today from their _____ _____ of
_____ .

8. When we do not sow the seeds, we _____ _____ have to
_____ the harvest _____ .
Do you really believe this? **YES/NO**

9. What is the sowing-and-reaping cycle that we are responsible to break?

_____

_____

_____

10. How does what happened to us years ago seem to live on today?

_____

11. What are these memories filled with?

_____

_____

12. What do they provide?

_____

_____

_____

13. What can neutralize the power of old memories?

_____

14. You can cooperate with your own _____ _____ by
_____ _____ the _____ and
_____ _____ that have _____ God any
_____ to the _____ _____ of your soul's
_____ .

15. God _____ _____ force His way into those areas.

16. What will happen when access is offered to Him?

_____

_____

_____

17. How can you cooperate by faith to give Him that access?

_____

_____

_____

Different Beginnings

18. All kinds of debits and credits were "posted to our human ledgers" before we were born. Name three possible liabilities the author listed.

_____

_____

_____

_____

Now, name three assets you believe were posted to your "human ledgers" before you were born, such as: intelligence, money, loving home, etc.

_____

_____

19. Without Jesus, you can spend your whole life trying to overcome _____ _____ or maybe just _____ to them and _____ _____ of the _____ entirely.

20. What was the first thing that happened when you became a Christian?

_____

21. Because of that, you no longer have to:
   a) Live under any liabilities from your natural heritage. **TRUE/FALSE**
   b) Figure out who you are based on your genes, psychological makeup, or your environment.
   TRUE/FALSE

22. What problem may you still have as a believer?

_____

_____

_____

23. Many believers have a flawed concept of their relationship with God because their view of Him is _____ by _____ _____.

24. How were these formed?

_____

25. Can you name two old mind sets that may be distorting your understanding of God?

_____

_____

26. Can you name three truly honest (rather than what you know you should say!) beliefs you have about God that don't exactly line up with your feeling like a special and precious child He loves?

_____

_____

_____

_____

27. What does God's view of us often produce in us?

_____

28. What causes us to have such a struggle?

_____

_____

_____

29. What might these filters be clogged with?

_____

30. What can happen in us because of what we have experienced in our past?

_____

_____

_____

_____

Everything you have ever _____ about God has had
to_____ _____ through
_____ _____, _____,
and _____ already _____ in your mind
_____ you ever knew Him.

---

31. Unless you know how to clean out the filters of your soul, wrong beliefs and attitudes can remain: (complete statement)

_____

_____

32. Will God's truth force its way through clogged filters of the mind? **YES/NO**

33. Scripturally correct teaching will automatically and immediately clear up wrong ideas you might have about God. **TRUE/FALSE**

34. What happens when you stop seeing yourself in terms of your past?

_____

_____

35. What then do you begin to recognize?

_____

_____

36. What begins to follow you everywhere you go?

_____

37. If you haven't seen that happening in your life—what has stopped it?

_____

_____

_____

38. The author says you should not "write off" the "troublemakers" in your church, at least not until they've remained so for decades. Instead, do what? Why?

_____

_____

_____

39. Do you know some "troublemakers" in your church, even in your personal life? Have you "written them off"? Are you willing to pray for God's will to be done in their lives, even if it means He blesses them and gives them opportunities you are still waiting for?

_____

_____

_____

_____

_____

40. Make a list and commit to remember them in prayer—see God change them and you in the process.

_____

_____

_____

_____

_____

> Be God's grace in action and don't give up on others!!

Enough of This Carnal Stuff!!!

41. Is your walk filled with powerless clichés and buzz words—in other words, things you keep saying so you sound spiritual, but you don't believe them yourself? **YES/NO**

42. Can you list some of the "phrases" you know you say, but don't always believe? Such as, "Of course I know God will do it." Or, "I've never felt disappointed in God." Or, "I know God loves me very much."

a)_____

b)_____

c)_____

d)_____

e)_____

43. Do you have a "form of Godliness," but no power? Have you lost hope that your life will ever change and get better?

_____

_____

_____

44. What seemingly radical words did the author pray for hours at a time to break out of that feeling?

_____

_____

_____

45. The author says it was a small breakthrough at first, but it kept breaking because she had given God a little _____ of access into her self-_____

_____ _____.

46. The opinionated, strong-willed author felt she had finally learned not to do what three things by the time the revelation began to unfold?

_____

_____

_____

She did what when those who knew her rejected the revelation she felt God was unfolding?

_____

_____

47. What did the two young women cry out the first night the author publicly preached this message?

_____

_____

48. What is the best answer to those who ask, "Why haven't we heard this before?"?

_____

_____

49. Matthew 16:19 tells us that Jesus said, "I will give unto _____ the

_____ of the _____ of _____ and

_____ thou shalt _____ on _____ shall

be _____ in _____ on earth _____ be

_____ in _____ " (KJV).

50. What does the word "whatsoever" cover?

_____

Truth and Faith is Powerful!

51. Who will be the new prayer warriors?

_____
_____
_____

52. What will they be free of?
a)_____
b)_____

53. Paul said in Hebrews 4:2 (AMP): "For indeed _____ have had the _____ tidings of God _____ to us as truly as they . . . but the message they heard did not _____ them, because it was _____ _____ _____ _____ (that is, with the leaning of the _____ _____ on God in _____ _____ and _____ in _____ _____ _____ and _____) by those who heard it."

54. If you don't act on these principles and make them yours, what will happen?

_____
_____
_____

55. What will happen if you do?

_____
_____

56. What will the words become?

_____
_____
_____

So Where Do You Begin?

57. What are some of the fruit of binding yourself to God's will?

_____
_____
_____

59. List the some of the binding principles of prayer you can pray immediately:
Binding . . .

   a)_____

   b)_____

   c)_____

   d)_____

   e)_____

   f)_____

59. James 4:3 (KJV) says, "Ye _____ [_____], and receive _____, because ye ask *amiss* . . ."

60. What does the Greek word for *amiss* mean?

61. How can you get all of your prayers answered every time?

Warning Bells and Whistles

62. Does binding your will to God's will mean you will behave perfectly from then on?

63. After binding your will to God's will, you have to deliberately choose to do what?

64. If we truly want God's will, what must we be willing to do?

65. What often happens when God brings something powerful but different into our lives?

66. When do we really put up a fuss?

67. Has God ever done something in your life that didn't match what you've "learned to expect" Him to do? What?

_____

_____

_____

_____

_____

68. What was the key to Mary's victory?

_____

_____

_____

69. What is it that cries out for security deposits and details when God stretches us?

_____

70. As God is working in our lives, our souls drive us to do what?

_____

_____

Supernatural and Practical

71. Truth won't do you any good if:

_____

_____

_____

72. Your mind _____ understand, nor is it _____ to
_____, _____ _____ God's Spirit.

73. The understanding of God's truth and trustworthiness can only be imparted into
_____ _____ by the _____
_____ of God.

74. What does your spirit want to do with the truth it receives from God?

_____

75. What thwarts this process?

_____

76. What can you do to prepare yourself to receive revelation truth from God?
   a)_____
   b)_____
   c)_____
   d)_____

77. When God gives you information that requires action, what must you do?

_____

78. Even though you have all of the knowledge and faith in the world, but you never act on it: (complete the statement)

_____

79. What are examples of taking an action of faith?

a)_____
_____

b)_____
_____

c)_____
_____

d)_____
_____

e)_____
_____

80. What is the next step after you have brought your soul into submission?

_____

81. How does faith grow and progress?

_____

82. Strongholds are designed to accomplish what purposes?

_____
_____

83. You will not act on or experience anything you have: (complete the statement)

_____

One Final Checkpoint!

84. What is your best defense against accepting a counterfeit?

_____
_____
_____

85. How important is it to fervently study false religions, cults, and New Age nuances? Why?

_____
_____
_____

86. What will happen when you are immersed in the Word of God and something phony comes along?

_____

_____

87. Looking back: What are the points in this chapter that especially touched a cord in you? Which ones stand out in your mind as affecting your life?

_____

_____

_____

_____

_____

88. Were there any points that made you angry, upset, or uncomfortable? If so, which ones?

_____

_____

_____

_____

_____

_____

REMEMBER: Your commitment to pray for yourself and others, and watch the transformation come forth.

Chapter 1 - Review

The most significant truths I found in this chapter are:

1. _____
   _____
   _____

2. _____
   _____
   _____

3. _____
   _____
   _____

4. _____
   _____
   _____

I applied these truths to my life as follows:

1. _____
   _____
   _____

2. _____
   _____
   _____

3. _____
   _____
   _____

4. _____
   _____
   _____

Chapter 1 - "Journey" Journal

Date: **Questions I have:**

Date: **Special insights I believe I have learned:**

Date: **Breakthroughs I have experienced:**

Chapter 1 - Prayer Journal

Date: **Prayer:**

Date: **Updates and special encouragements I've received from the Lord:**

Date: **Answers to prayers:**

2
Body, Soul, Spirit, and Strongholds

1. God designed you to function as a _____-_____ _____ consisting of a _____, _____, and a _____.

2. How does your body relate to its environment?

_____

_____

3. When all your body's needs are met, what will it do?

_____

_____

4. Your spirit is that part of you that relates to God's Spirit. What is your spirit's desire?

_____

5. When you asked Jesus Christ to forgive you and wash you in His blood, what happened to your spirit?

_____

_____

6. Your soul is made up of your _____, _____, and _____.

7. Your soul is meant to be in perfect alignment with _____ _____ and purposes.

8. The soul strongly resists _____ or _____.

9. The soul wants to be the final word on all "system" decisions, overruling what?

_____

_____

10. In the beginning, God's Spirit communicated through _____
_____ to His _____ which jointly _____
_____, or manifested, God's _____ _____
through man's _____.

11. After the fall in the Garden of Eden, what happened to man's spirit?

_____
_____

12. Man's spirit lost what?

_____
_____

Man's soul did what?

_____
_____

> "I believe the human spirits of all men and women ever since the fall have felt lost, helpless, and needy, just like spiritual orphans, wanting only to be reunited with their Creator's Spirit."

13. On page 19, the author shares a story to illustrate what point?

_____
_____

14. Your soul wants to defend what?

_____

15. What do strongholds do?

_____
_____
_____

16. What happens because God will not cross the walls of the soul's inner strongholds?

_____

17. Satan always shows up to do what?

_____
_____
_____

18. The wounded, needy soul can be hammered by evil spirits when the _____
_____ is in control.

The Real Rebel

19. When you accepted Jesus Christ as your Savior, what part of you actually got saved?

_____

20. What did your unsurrendered soul do?

_____

_____

21. What does man's unsurrendered soul want?

_____

22. A lot of money can be made off the _____ _____

_____ .

23. What is one major reason the world is not eager to cater to God's plan?

_____

24. Philippians 2:12 (AMP) speaks of the ongoing process of the soul's salvation:
" . . . Work out—cultivate, _____ _____ to the goal and
_____ _____ - your own _____ with
reverence and awe and trembling (self-distrust, that is, with serious _____, tenderness
of conscience, _____ against _____ ; timidly
_____ from whatever might _____ God and
_____ the name of Christ)."

25. What does 2 Corinthians 10:5 (KJV) tell us?

_____

_____

_____

26. What does Thayer's Greek/English Lexicon say about this?

_____

_____

_____

27. What do our souls do to keep us from having a true knowledge of God? Can you name one example of such soulish resistance that has kept you from an area of complete surrender to God?

_____

_____

_____

_____

_____

28. What is our spirit-man's job description?

_____

_____

_____

Why Do We Build Strongholds?

29. Why do we build strongholds in the first place?

_____

_____

30. What do they allow us to do?

_____

31. What happens when a child is badly abused by a parent?

_____

32. Young children do not have the emotional and mental capabilities to process emotional, mental, and physical abuse and betrayal. Because of this lack, what do they do?

_____

33. This is the beginning of what twisted reasoning that many Christians even retain?

_____

_____

_____

34. How does this incorrect reasoning seem to "logically" play out?

_____

_____

35. This type of reasoning also exists in:

_____

_____

36. Have you ever said, "If I hadn't done this, or if I hadn't said that, he/she wouldn't have done such and such"? Do you see the error of this stronghold thinking? If not, go back to question 33.

_____

37. Such thinking will always impair your life until you do what?

_____

38. When do we become static and stop growing?

_____

_____

39. What will keep us from becoming who God says we can be?

_____

40. What roles should we have moved into when we came to Christ?
  a)_____
  b)_____
  c)_____
  _____

41. Why have our souls stopped us from doing so? Can you name one of the areas you know is still impacting your life?

_____
_____
_____
_____

Preventive Soul Maintenance

42. What are causes for great alarm in the unsurrendered soul?

_____

43. What do these intense feelings initiate in the unsurrendered soul?

_____

44. Be very aware when someone offends, insults, lies, or tricks you so that you do not respond with indignation and anger to the offense. Why?

_____
_____
_____
_____

45. Self-righteous anger should not be confused with _____ _____

46. Explain the difference between the anger of Moses and the anger of Jesus.

_____
_____
_____

47. What must we always keep in mind regarding our anger?

_____

48. What must you not do (a) so you can do what (b) to pull your emotions and thoughts back into alignment with God's will?
  a)_____
  b)_____
  _____

49. What other three things should you do?

_____

_____

_____

50. What is self-righteous anger a result of?

_____

_____

_____

51. When is anger never godly?

_____

_____

52. What is your soul the master of?

_____

53. What might some of its rationalization sound like?

_____

_____

54. What is your soul's internal chant?

_____

55. What happens as your soul attempts to enforce this dogma?

_____

_____

56. What is a word picture of this soulish process?

_____

_____

_____

What God Won't Do For You

57. What do you build self-protective strongholds out of?

_____

58. No matter how hard you pray, God will not do what for you?

_____

_____

59. What will He do?

_____

_____

_____

60. Why do some resist using the binding and loosing training wheel prayers?

_____

_____

61. Are there written prayers in the Bible? **YES/NO**

62. Write out 2 Timothy 3:16 (KJV) here.

_____

_____

_____

63. Does the above verse include any written prayers in the Bible, too? (Read Ephesians 3:14-21.)

_____

64. What kind of prayers would God have a problem with? _____

_____.

65. The word "vain" used by Jesus in Matthew 6:7 defines what kind of prayers?

_____

_____

66. Binding and loosing prayers squeeze what?

_____

67. What is a "good word" regarding how we should pray?

_____

68. Pray _____ _____, _____
_____ prayer, _____ _____ prayer,
_____ _____ _____ prayer, pray
_____ _____ from the Bible.

69. As you pray your usual prayers, add in some form of:

_____

_____

_____

70. The author says she has experienced what five things as she has continued tearing down and tearing up strongholds, large and small?

_____

_____

_____

_____

Got Any Struggles?

71. How do you know if you have a surrendered or an unsurrendered soul? List at least ten sure signs the author lists:

_____

_____

_____

_____

_____

_____

_____

_____

_____

_____

72. Get the picture? Add any personal struggles you are experiencing:

_____

_____

_____

_____

73. How does God help us recognize when we are operating out of unsurrendered souls?

_____

_____

_____

74. Even though we might think He has forsaken us; He is actually very close. What is He waiting for?

_____

_____

_____

The Vehicles are Driving Themselves

75. Left to his devices, what will man usually do?

_____
_____
_____

76. What is he trying to accomplish in doing this?

_____
_____

77. What is the problem with this man-made theory of self-attainment?

_____
_____
_____

78. Where does true peace, satisfaction, and joy come from?

_____

79. Unshakable, unchanging peace, and joy are found in: (circle one)
    a) knowing ourselves better
    b) knowing Jesus better

80. How can deep introspection, focused on inner fact finding trips, be dangerous?

_____
_____

81. Some false "memories" seem so real, only two sources of truth can reveal their deception. Name them:

_____

82. What is the purpose of the soul?

_____
_____

83. What was it designed to do?

_____
_____

84. When our soul attempts to drive our lives, what occurs?

_____
_____
_____

85. A lot of _____ _____ is _____ when we
_____ _____ _____ out of the
_____ _____ and leave the _____ to God.

86. When we allow our souls to control our lives, we set ourselves up for what two things?
_____

87. What is the training-wheel prayer designed to do?
_____
_____

Stop now and pray the Training-Wheel Prayer for Breaking Soul Power on page 30.

Who's Taking Authority Here?

88. Where do fear and unbelief reside?
_____

89. Which part of you "takes authority" over anything?
_____

90. All three parts of an unsurrendered soul are determined to do what?
_____
_____

91. Your soul is not going to do what?
_____
_____

92. What part of you will God take authority over?
_____

93. What can you do to achieve victory over your will?
_____

94. What does the author say has been the main challenge from the unsurrendered souls to the binding and loosing prayers?
_____
_____

95. What are today's Christians quick to defend?
_____

But I Just Don't Know What God Wants

96. Where is everything recorded that we would ever need to know?

_____

97. Our spirits are eager to respond to His will and His Word. Our souls are the part of us that always make Christianity seem so difficult. What do our souls want to do (a) and look for (b) in a religion?

a)_____

_____

b)_____

_____

98. Galatians 5:16 (AMP) says in part: "Walk and live _____ in the (Holy Spirit)— _____ to and _____ and _____ by the Spirit.

99. What is the unsurrendered soul adamant about?

_____

_____

_____

100. What must we do to be completely controlled and guided by God's Spirit?

_____

_____

_____

101. Our unsurrendered souls do not want to do anything God's easy way. They want what?

_____

_____

102. If our souls won't surrender, what might God have to do?

_____

_____

_____

103. One encouragement we have is that greatness in God sometimes results from very

_____, _____-_____,

_____-_____ kinds of _____ in

_____ _____. So, take heart if your life seems like such a

_____ _____.

104. If you are in the middle of a spiritual war zone, what should you do?

_____

_____

_____

105. Hebrews 5:14 (AMP) tells us that spiritual meat eaters are: "Those whose senses and mental faculties are _____ _____ practice to _____ and _____ between what is _____ _____ and _____ and what is _____ and _____ either to divine or human law."

106. What good does unconditional support, love, and compassion accomplish in a struggling life?

_____

_____

_____

107. What hindrances can a perpetuation of this "good" cause?

_____

108. What does John 8:32 say about the truth?

_____

109. Why do many of those who are spiritually "unripe" or immature often pour so much love and mercy out to those around them?

_____

_____

110. What are these same believers often incapable of?

_____

_____

111. The One who loves best loves with a perfect balance of what two things?

_____

112. Look up John 1:14 in your favorite version of Scripture and record here:

_____

_____

_____

_____

Getting Close to God

113. What will your soul do if it cannot get you to cast off all thoughts of God?

_____

_____

114. What might it push you into?

_____

_____

_____

_____

115. What is very easy to slip into in the ministry?

_____
_____
_____

116. God is not interested in anything you do for Him if: (complete the statement)

_____

> Your soul can be glorying in what you are "doing" for God, while your spirit can be starving at the exact same time because of lack of intimacy with God.

Hebrews 12:1 says: "Therefore, since we are surrounded by such a cloud of witnesses, let us throw off everything that hinders and the sin that so easily entangles, and let us run with perseverance the race marked out for us" (NIV).

117. The word sin in this verse comes from the Greek word *hamartia*. What is its general meaning?

_____

118. Entangled or beset in the original Greek means:

_____
_____

119. What might you need to lay aside that may "be good" but not God?

_____
_____
_____
_____
_____
_____

120. Ask yourself if you are more comfortable with "doing things for" or "spending time with" God.

_____

121. Why are our souls more interested in "doing things for" God?

_____
_____

122. If you need to make a priority change, write it out here and date it so you will have a record of choosing to do so. You may need to refer to it at times as a remembrance.

DATE:_____ COMMITMENT:_____

_____
_____
_____

Chapter 2 - Review

The most significant truths I found in this chapter are:

1. _____
_____
_____

2. _____
_____
_____

3. _____
_____
_____

4. _____
_____
_____

I applied these truths to my life as follows:

1. _____
_____
_____

2. _____
_____
_____

3. _____
_____
_____

4. _____
_____
_____

Chapter 2 - "Journey" Journal

Date: **Questions I have:**

Date: **Special insights I believe I have learned:**

Date: **Breakthroughs I have experienced:**

Chapter 2 - Prayer Journal

Date: **Prayer:**

Date: **Updates and special encouragements I've received from the Lord:**

Date: **Answers to prayers:**

3
Satanic/Soulish Deception of the Church

1. What "mixture" is the church world currently struggling with in trying to help the hurting?

_____

2. The good news of the Gospel remains very straightforward and simple. What is it?

_____
_____
_____

3. What do we need to release or loose to make room to receive the rights of our relationship with Christ?

_____
_____
_____

4. We desperately need to understand that Jesus really wants _____ to be
_____! (After filling in the blanks, read aloud at least five times.)

5. Why have we not pursued understanding on how to open ourselves to God's healing grace?

_____

Artificial Life Support

6. How is our pain kept alive?

_____
_____

7. How do our souls dictate the terms of our healing process?

_____
_____

8. How do our souls reinforce emotional leverage?

_____

_____

9. Your soul believes it has stored all of the necessary facts of your unresolved injustices in your memory. It is just trying to do what now?

_____

_____

10. Why do self-help books and programs about self-empowerment intrigue the untransformed mind?

_____

_____

11. Digging up and prioritizing the who and the what of your past is important to the answer of your healing. **TRUE/FALSE**

12. What does divine grace require you to do to be healed?

_____

_____

_____

13. What two things will grace help with?

_____

_____

_____

14. What will your soul do as you move toward God? Why does it do this?

_____

_____

_____

15. What must you do?

_____

_____

Just Give Up

16. What will the binding and loosing prayers do?

_____

_____

_____

17. In so doing, the facts still exist—but what happens?

_____

_____

18. What is your part in this process?

_____

_____

19. What must we do to become useful, strong, productive Christians?

_____

_____

_____

20. We should _____ _____ _____ and _____ to work because _____ says they _____.

21. Why must we stop building protective strongholds around erroneous, worldly principles?
    a)_____
    b)_____
    c)_____

22. You must prevent your soul from blocking out what solution?

_____

Here a Spirit, There a Spirit

23. That which you might think is a "controlling spirit" in a believer is generally what?

_____

_____

_____

_____

24. That which you might think is an "unteachable spirit" in a believer is generally what?

_____

_____

_____

_____

25. A believer you might think has a "Jezebel spirit" is really a person with a:

_____

26. The label "Jezebel spirit" has been used to do what (a) to many who seem to be what (b)?
    a)_____
    b)_____

27. Such carnality in a believer is not the work of an evil spirit, but a soul driven by:

_____

_____

28. What has contributed to so much emphasis on evil spirits rather than an emphasis on the believer's old nature?

_____

_____

_____

29. If we can blame our shortcomings on evil spirits, what does this mean to us?

_____

_____

_____

30. What is the bottom line error in this misplaced trust in deliverance?

_____

31. Why have so many thrown themselves into wrong spiritual fights?

_____

_____

_____

32. It seems logical to fight what you have been told _____ _____

_____.

33. Why do few tell you how to win the battle with your internal foe, your unsurrendered soul?

_____

How We Have Missed the Truth

34. Name the reason why so many Christians are willing to believe so many doctrines about so many evil spirits:

_____

_____

35. What two books does author believe can help anyone do Hebrew research of the Old Testament?

_____

_____

36. Psalm 51:16-17 (KJV), "For thou desirest not _____; else would I give it; thou delightest _____ in _____ offering. The sacrifices of God are a _____ _____; a _____ and a _____ _____, O God, thou _____ _____ despise."

37. The word "spirit" as used here comes from the Hebrew word *ruwach*. In this specific verse, *ruwach* means:

_____

_____

38. What does this meaning refer to?

_____

39. The word "heart," as used in this verse, comes from the Hebrew word *lebab* which Gesenius describes as:

_____
_____
_____

40. This word is closely related to *leb* which Strongs describes as:

_____
_____

41. The word contrite or *dakah*, as used in this verse, means:

_____
_____

42. This reference to the contrite heart means a broken and crushed soul. What does this also describe?

_____
_____
_____

43. In *The Message*, Psalm 51:16-17 reads, "Going through the _____
_____ _____ _____, a
_____ _____ is nothing to you. I learned
_____ - _____ when my _____
_____ _____. _____
_____ _____ _____ ready for love
_____ for a moment _____ _____
_____.''

44. Isaiah 61:3 refers to a spirit of heaviness. What does the NIV call this?

_____
_____

45. Rather than describing a troubling spirit, what is the word spirit, as used here, really describing?

_____
_____
_____

46. What else does this verse refer to (according to Gesenius)?

_____

47. Proverbs 25:28 tells us that he who has no rule over his own spirit is like what?

_____

48. How is the original Hebrew meaning of the word spirit, *ruwach*, used in this Scripture?

_____

_____

49. Therefore, a man who has no rule over his own soul is like:

_____

50. Isaiah 19:14 speaks of a perverse spirit which Gesenius renders *ruwach* to mean in this verse:

_____

_____

51. What does this meaning imply about the phrase used here as "perverse spirit"?

_____

_____

52. Hosea 4:12 speaks of the spirit of whoredoms. The word spirit as used here means:

_____

_____

53. Many so-called evil spirits spoken of in the church world cannot be found in the Bible as actual entities. Rather, they are descriptive adjectives used to identify attitudes of an unsurrendered soul. Name at least eight of these wrong soulish "attitudes."

_____

_____

_____

_____

_____

_____

54. Evil spirits _____ _____, _____ _____, and they are _____ _____. But a _____, _____, _____ believer does not have to war with them for the _____ _____ of his own _____.

55. In Philippians 2:12, how is the working out of your salvation explained?

_____

_____

56. Where does the believer's strength lie?

_____

_____

57. Using the truth in Matthew 16:19 will help close doors of access in the soul and neutralize what?

_____

_____

_____

58. What are evil spirits drawn to?

_____

59. When doors of access are available to them, wrong spirits can compound what?

_____

There are Genuine Evil Spirits

60. In Leviticus 20:27, the familiar spirit refered to is a:

_____

61. First Samuel 16:14 tells us an evil spirit from the Lord troubled King Saul. How does this happen?

_____

_____

62. God is never out of _____ of _____,

_____, _____!

63. What has caused many to build an entire structure of spiritual warfare based on false premises?

_____

_____

Spiritual or Secular Psychology?

64. What are three of the counterfeit "manifestations" of the unsurrendered soul?

_____

_____

65. What three forms of help have failed to produce permanent healing in troubled souls?

_____

_____

66. What has bolstered the soul's position as the gatekeeper to the source of a believer's problem?

_____

Repressed Memory Syndrome

67. When spiritual counseling/secular psychological help creates a hybrid form of therapy that goes awry, we must be spiritually realistic and not paint all of these backlashes as what two things?

_____

_____

68. There are recorded instances of many counselors, some even Christian, who have used secular techniques to supposedly uncover "repressed memories" of abuse in order to do what?

_____

_____

> Sometimes a terrified, wounded, angry soul creates a psychological deception to validate its fear and hopelessness.

Multiple Personality Disorder

69. What prayer example does the author give of how she ministered to the women "displaying" MPD symptoms?

_____

_____

_____

70. We will never achieve permanent solutions and healing for wounded souls by: (complete the statement)

_____

_____

_____

Wounded Inner Child

71. What does the "wounded inner child" deception allow?

_____

_____

72. Those who accept this deception and believe they have a wounded, inner victim/child suffer from what?

_____

_____

_____

73. The woman mentioned in the wounded inner child section of this chapter agreed to do what three things to overcome this deception her soul was embracing?

_____

_____

_____

_____

_____

74. Formerly, when family members did not respond to her efforts as she expected and desired them to, what happened in her and in her family members?

_____

_____

_____

_____

_____

75. Can you think of similar examples in your family relationships?

_____

_____

_____

76. When she later approached her family at the next holiday with no preconceived expectations, positive or negative, what happened?

_____

_____

_____

The Secular World's Victim Manufacturing Industry

77. Dr. Dineen says secular psychology has become an _____ and her colleagues have been _____ _____ and _____

_____.

78. Dr. Dineen only had one problem with religious counselors. What was it?

_____

_____

_____

79. Too many secular-inspired counseling techniques fit over what?

_____

_____

80. The Church must return to its roots of using what?

_____

_____

_____

81. We must return to teaching and practicing the scriptural truth of what two things as the only sources of healing and wholeness?

_____

_____

82. Per 2 Corinthians 10:4-5 (AMP), our God-given weapons are for what?

_____

_____

_____

_____

_____

_____

Formula Answers, No Answers, or Wrong Answers

83. Why do many ministers and leaders give formula answers, no answers, or wrong answers?

_____

_____

_____

84. God's healing grace can seem totally abstract to who?

_____

_____

_____

85. Your spiritual position as a member of God's family can be invalidated by behavior you are struggling to overcome. **TRUE/FALSE**

86. The validity of our salvation experience can be "determined" by human judgment calls on wrong behavior we have not yet overcome. **TRUE/FALSE**

87. How can we create a spiritual safety net for those who are falling?

_____

_____

_____

_____

So Many Trials and Tribulations

88. Christians struggling and torn between spiritual hunger and worldly crutches usually have two factors present in their lives. What are they?

_____

_____

_____

_____

89. It is sad, but sometimes believers perceive trials and tribulations as what?

_____

90. Some believers on the "Potter's Wheel" adopt a victim mentality. They may use it to what?

_____

91. Why do they do this?

_____
_____
_____
_____

92. In using binding and loosing principles to cooperate with God, what should be the motive of your prayers?

_____
_____
_____

He Must Increase, I Must Decrease (John 3:30)

93. What must decrease?

_____

94. What does the basic law of physics tell us?

_____

95. Before He can increase, what must happen?

_____
_____

96. We do not always recognize new facets of revelation from God. We may even reject them if we can't what?

_____
_____

97. If you have a strong sense of what you have already been taught about spiritual warfare, what question should you still ask yourself?

_____
_____

98. What do we do to protect ourselves from what we perceive to be our external enemies?

_____
_____
_____

99. We are what kind of creatures?

_____

100. We believe God needs us to do what to the devil?

_____

_____

101. Is this true? **YES/NO**

_____

God Does Do Roadblocks

102. What will the soul do if left unchallenged?

_____

_____

103. Why?

_____

_____

104. Why does God set up roadblocks?

_____

_____

105. How do we know that God knows what's best for us? Jeremiah 29:11 tells us that God has said, "I know the _____ I have for _____, declares the _____, plans to _____ you and _____ to _____ you, plans to give you _____ and a _____."

Chapter 3 - Review

The most significant truths I found in this chapter are:

1. _____
_____
_____

2. _____
_____
_____

3. _____
_____
_____

4. _____
_____
_____

I applied these truths to my life as follows:

1. _____
_____
_____

2. _____
_____
_____

3. _____
_____
_____

4. _____
_____
_____

Chapter 3 - "Journey" Journal

Date: **Questions I have:**

Date: **Special insights I believe I have learned:**

Date: **Breakthroughs I have experienced:**

Chapter 3 - Prayer Journal

Date: **Prayer:**

Date: **Updates and special encouragements I've received from the Lord:**

Date: **Answers to prayers:**

4
Wrong Behaviors, Word Curses, and Generational Bondages

1. Some believers try to serve Jesus while packing what around?

_____

_____

2. What does the church world today often choose to employ while counseling?

_____

_____

_____

3. What is God's heart's message to every hurting lamb who feels hopelessly entangled in sin and wrong behaviors?

_____

_____

_____

_____

_____

4. God's Word covers every kind of what?

_____

_____

How the Church Views Wrong Behavior

5. How does legalism begin to creep into teachings in the Church?

_____

_____

_____

6. What lack of understanding can cause even sincere Christians to fail?

_____

_____

_____

7. What do some believers do when they get discouraged over failure?

_____

_____

8. When a believer is afraid of being exposed and called a hypocrite, what will he or she do?

_____

_____

9. Most Christians can modify some of their wrong behaviors, disguise them, and temporarily bury them. These "front line" defense measures will eventually surface when?

_____

_____

10. The answer to this dilemma resides in:

_____

_____

11. Is self-denial ever a permanent solution? **YES/NO**

12. What is self-denial?

_____

_____

13. When a change in behavior comes from a soulish agenda, the soul has usually decided what?

_____

_____

_____

14. A change in circumstances that brings about a termination of a benefit the soul has perceived will cause what to happen?

_____

_____

15. What kind of behavior is not altered by a change in circumstances?

_____

_____

Outward Behaviors Have Inward Sources

16. No one, either devil or human, can get a Christian to do any wrong thing he doesn't already have an inward source driving him towards. **TRUE/FALSE**

17. The devil will do all he can to help us destroy ourselves in our self-efforts to do what three things?

_____

_____

18. List the two examples given of his tactics to see the above accomplished:

_____

_____

19. If no understanding or hope is available to guide them, what might very needy people do?

_____

_____

20. When a self-destructive behavior produces temporary relief, what can temporarily lighten the load of related pain and shame?

_____

21. What will the power sources of our old natures torment us with?

_____

_____

22. How do wrong behaviors generally begin?

_____

_____

_____

23. The author believes homosexual and lesbian lifestyles begin how?

_____

_____

> Someone in the homosexual lifestyle was present at just the "right time" to reach out and comfort someone else whose unmet needs were overwhelming.

24. What causes someone to automatically feel the need to justify and rationalize homosexual behavior?

_____

_____

25. What does this rationalization and justification process cause to happen?

_____

_____

_____

26. What happens when this rationalization process is repeated?

_____

_____

_____

27. When the devil has a foothold through personal strongholds, our sinful "coping" behaviors are driven by what two sources?

_____
_____
_____
_____

28. You must _____ your soul's strongholds to give the _____

_____ _____ into _____

_____ _____ _____

_____ . This is your part. The Holy Spirit _____

_____ _____ .

Natural Strategies Won't Win Spiritual Fights

29. What is the beginning of permanent freedom?

_____

30. What causes many wrong behaviors to fall away and evil spirits to run away?

_____

31. When religious rules and regulations are the only behavioral backup a soul has, what happens with the wrong behaviors and the evil spirits?

_____
_____
_____
_____

32. Christian behavior modification: (choose one)
   a) changes wrong behaviors
   b) repositions wrong behaviors

33. You cannot _____ pure thinking. You can only _____

_____ _____ .

34. How do you move your thoughts out of the realm of your soul's control and into Christ-like thinking?

_____
_____

35. When I use the Kingdom key of loosing in regard to having wrong thoughts, I need to do what three things?

_____
_____
_____
_____

Coping Techniques

36. What does modifying a wrong behavior do?

_____
_____

37. How do coping techniques "work"?

_____
_____

38. When you repeatedly refuse to let God into your needs that you are "controlling" with a coping behavior, things can get rough. How?

_____
_____
_____

39. What will you generally do when coping behaviors are your means of resisting external temptations?

_____
_____
_____

40. What does this conflict with?

_____

41. _____ _____ in your _____ stand between _____ and _____.

42. This gives Satan a legal right to do what?

_____

43. What is the second smartest choice you can make as a believer?

_____
_____
_____

44. What is the first smartest choice?

_____

45. What can Jesus permanently do?

_____

Heritage Hindrances

46. Isaiah 54:17 says, "_____ _____ that is _____ against thee _____ _____, and every _____ that shall _____ _____ _____ in _____ thou shalt _____. This is the _____ of the _____ of the Lord, and their _____ is of me, saith the Lord."

47. What would stop the protection from tongues of judgment rising up against a Christian?

_____
_____
_____
_____
_____

48. What do some believers believe about claiming scriptural promises?

_____
_____
_____
_____
_____

49. What frequently bolsters this kind of thinking?

_____
_____

50. What kind of thinking does Satan love, knowing it prevents us from determining the real source of our problems?

_____
_____
_____
_____
_____

51. Ezekiel 28 speaks of the guardian cherub who was created beautiful, perfect, and with great wisdom. Who was that?

_____

52. Did he lose his superior intelligence when he was thrown out of heaven? **YES/NO**

53. Is Satan smarter than Christians who have genius mental capabilities? **YES/NO**

54. Why would God strive with a person?

_____

_____

_____

55. What is the hardest way surrender sometimes comes about?

_____

56. Firewalls are generally accompanied by what by the time they fall?

_____

57. In the spiritual realm, what are your firewalls?

_____

58. What might God allow in a life to bring these dangerous "firewalls" down?

_____

And the Beat Goes On

59. What is the key to deliverance from wrong behaviors?

_____

60. To what can we relate the strength of our bondage to wrong behavior?

_____

61. Our shame over our wrong behaviors and needs comes from God being angry with us. **TRUE/FALSE**

62. God has given us truth all through the Word about how to cooperate with His doing what?

_____

_____

63. Where does the ongoing pain from your past exist?

_____

64. What terminates your soul's artificial "life support system" regarding your memories?

_____

65. What happened to you years ago has no real life today unless you do what?

_____

_____

66. When you choose to expose the source of your pain's "life," what happens?

_____

_____

67. What then happens to the "bad" memories?

_____

_____

_____

Systems Versus Sources

68. Why do some of our prayers go unanswered?

_____

69. Instead of shattering the strongholds protecting the source of the problems, what do we often pray about instead?

_____

70. What does focusing on symptoms keep us from doing?

_____

71. What is Satan's only edge over you as a believer?

_____

72. How has he been using them against you?

_____

_____

> What good is accomplished if God removes an existing desire for drugs or any sin when the source fueling these behaviors and desires still exist?

73. What will sources continue to do if not dealt with?

_____

74. Why don't we have to name the symptoms or identify specific sources?

_____

75. Why do our prayers for our loved ones remain unanswered?

_____

_____

Learning to Pray Right Prayers

76. When your body is attacked with symptoms of illness, what should you pray?

_____

_____

77. If it were a spiritual attack, what would you do?

_____

_____

78. What was the problem with the author's "flu" attack, and what did she do?

_____

_____

_____

_____

79. Open doors in your soul can have what effect on your body?

_____

_____

80. When a Christian's body, soul, and spirit get out of God's desired alignment, what happens?

_____

81. Other people speaking wrong words about us can be the result of Satan pressuring them how?

_____

_____

82. What would be a case of strongholds spawning strongholds?

_____

_____

_____

_____

83. "Like a fluttering sparrow or a darting swallow, an undeserved curse does not come to rest" (Proverbs 26:2, NIV). A curse that is not deserved can only find a landing place when?

_____

84. _____ and _____ to God's Word remove any

_____ _____ _____.

Word Curses

85. What are the primary sources of wrong behavior?
   a)_____
   b)_____
   c)_____

86. What is a secondary source of wrong behaviors?

_____

_____

87. When can an occultic, demonic word curse be cast upon a Christian?

_____

88. Natural spoken _____ _____ bring about
_____ _____ for more _____ than
demonic curses.

89. What word curses have no expiration dates unless they are challenged?

_____

90. What is the main thing you need to know about natural word curses?

_____
_____

91. What might some natural word curses sound like?

_____
_____
_____
_____
_____

92. Have any natural word curses been spoken to you? List them.

_____
_____
_____
_____
_____
_____

93. How will you see everything in life if your soul agrees with word curses as truth?

_____
_____

94. Such words spoken cannot be erased, but you can do what?

_____

95. You must know what has been spoken against you before you can loose the words' effects.
TRUE/FALSE

Healing

96. The same principle of deconstructing the power of word curses impacting your beliefs and attitudes
DOES/DOES NOT apply to your health. (circle one)

97. Even in the presence of natural symptoms, the author always looses what?

_____

_____

98. How can sickness and disease remain in our bodies?

_____

_____

99. What will your body come into alignment with?

_____

_____

_____

_____

100. What will your soul use to escape dealing with something it fears it cannot handle?

_____

_____

101. If you frequently get "sick" whenever stress and pressure intensifies in your life, what may be happening?

_____

_____

_____

Is There a Sign on the Back Bumper of My Car?

102. When educated prognoses were given to the author after her fifth rear-end auto accident, what did she overlook?

_____

_____

103. Have authority figures spoken negative words into your life? List examples:

_____

_____

_____

_____

_____

104. What did the author need to do to step into God's unlimited reality?

_____

_____

105. The author moved out of and into what two modes of thinking?

_____

_____

_____

Reality, Hope or Denial

106. What must we sometimes do in order to walk into the plans God has for the rest of our lives?

_____

_____

_____

107. Why do some people seem unable to get over traumatic things?

_____

_____

_____

108. What can cause us to have little hope for getting well?

_____

_____

109. What always happens when binding and loosing prayers are prayed in the right manner and with faith?

_____

_____

110. When specialists in a medical field agree on a diagnosis and plan of treatment, what two things do we need to remember?

_____

_____

111. Your body will follow whatever or whoever seems to be in control of your belief systems. Why?

_____

_____

_____

112. This need is so strong that the human body will do what to itself to come into alignment with intellectual and emotional wrong agreements existing in your soul?

_____

_____

113. Medical science has proven what about persistent fears of getting a specific disease?

_____

_____

_____

114. What is the positive side of this incredible ability of the human body?

_____

_____

_____

_____

> Have you entered into wrong agreement with and accepted wrong beliefs about your health?

115. List any possible wrong agreements, wrong generational beliefs, or conventional wisdom you have accepted as truth with regard to your physical health.

_____

_____

_____

_____

_____

_____

116. What depends upon your knowing whether your soul or spirit is in charge of your belief systems?

_____

> If He is in control and you are bound to His will, you will be in the palm of His hand—whatever happens.

117. Does the unknown possibility of the phrase "whatever happens" frighten you? **YES/NO**

> If you answered yes, recognize that your health is not the problem. A lack of trust in God's good plans is the problem.

"Generational-Bondage" Thinking

118. What is another secondary source of wrong behaviors?

_____

119. How does Webster describe in part the word heredity?

_____

_____

120. What does the author say is most responsible for passing on of generational bondage?

_____

_____

121. If there are strong areas of anger, unforgiveness, impatience, and/or mistrust in an unsurrendered soul, what will that person's verbal expressions sound like?

_____

122. What will almost always be shared when people are repeatedly put together in close quarters?

_____

_____

Christian Families in Bondage

123. Actual spiritual generational bondage does occur. It can be passed from a non-believing generation to a Christian generation. How?

_____

124. Does a marriage ceremony in a big church automatically close the doors on wrong spirits that have known access to individual's souls? **YES/NO**

125. Will a marriage ceremony turn lust into godly sexual desire? **YES/NO**

126. How will the doors of access be closed that were previously opened through the couple's prior acts of fornication?

a)_____

_____

b)_____

_____

c)_____

_____

d)_____

_____

127. When this hypothetical couple has a child, what may surface in the child if no closing of doors of access in the parents' lives has been accomplished?

_____

_____

128. What other reasons might cause this abnormal behavior in a child of a Christian couple?

_____

_____

129. Because of never having been taught about their souls' disorder and misalignment and strongholds, what might be the outcome of this hypothetical family's story?

_____

_____

_____

Chapter 4 - Review

The most significant truths I found in this chapter are:

1. _____
_____
_____

2. _____
_____
_____

3. _____
_____
_____

4. _____
_____
_____

I applied these truths to my life as follows:

1. _____
_____
_____

2. _____
_____
_____

3. _____
_____
_____

4. _____
_____
_____

Chapter 4 - "Journey" Journal

Date: **Questions I have:**

Date: **Special insights I believe I have learned:**

Date: **Breakthroughs I have experienced:**

Chapter 4 - Prayer Journal

Date: **Prayer:**

Date: **Updates and special encouragements I've received from the Lord:**

Date: **Answers to prayers:**

5
Unmet Needs, Unhealed Hurts, Unresolved Issues

1. All of us have needs we have given up expecting any fulfillment of, hurts that still ache years after they are inflicted, and troubling issues we've never been able to understand. What do we usually learn to do to try to deal with these feelings?

a)_____

b)_____

c)_____

d)_____

e)_____

f)_____

2. Why do we do this?

_____

3. Does it make us happy? Why not?

_____

_____

4. What does our life seem to be consumed with today?

a)_____

b)_____

c)_____

d)_____

5. How can we end up feeling in our reactions to this heavy load?

_____

_____

6. What do we then do?

_____

_____

7. What would the perfect case scenario have been as we were growing up?

_____
_____
_____
_____
_____
_____
_____

8. Why didn't this happen?

_____
_____
_____

9. What factor prevents this from happening right now?

_____

Your Soul's First Line of Defense

10. What is the first line of defense of your unsurrendered soul against any interference with it's position of power in your life?

_____

11. Built from what?
    a)_____
    b)_____
    c)_____
    d)_____
    e)_____
    f)_____

Which are guarding the wrong:
    a)_____
    b)_____
    c)_____
    d)_____
    e)_____

12. If your soul can keep you trapped by these strongholds, what will you never do?

_____
_____

13. Where does Satan and your unsurrendered soul do battle?

_____

14. Write out Romans 12:2 (AMP) and then circle what you consider to be the five most important words.

_____
_____
_____
_____
_____
_____

15. When strongholds are being shattered, what begins to become visible?

_____
_____

Facts Cannot Be Loosed

17. Can you change the factual events of your childhood? **YES/NO**

18. Facts _____ _____ loosed.

19. Because of the errors of omission in your early life, what was birthed in your soul?
    a)_____
    b)_____
    c)_____

20. These areas of vulnerability produce what? Which keeps you from what?

_____
_____
_____

21. Why does your soul use the outworkings of your vulnerabilities?

_____
_____

22. What are these outworkings?

_____
_____
_____

23. Explain why you think the author said to Mark, "You leak!"

_____
_____
_____
_____

24. What are like bottomless holes in your soul?

_____

_____

25. What or who is the only way we can fill up the gaping holes these things leave?

_____

26. List the things our souls try to convince us as being good substitutes or "hole" fillers:

a)_____

b)_____

c)_____

d)_____

e)_____

f)_____

g)_____

27. What lies right above the soul's unmet needs, unhealed hurts, and unresolved issues?

_____

_____

28. There are two ways the power structure of the soul can be deconstructed. Explain them:

THE BAD WAY:

_____

_____

_____

_____

THE GOOD WAY:

_____

_____

_____

_____

29. What does God pour into the voluntarily unblocked soul?

_____

_____

30. What is the hopeful purpose of this book?

_____

_____

Our Part

31. Why do we come into this world with a strong sense of darkness?

_____

32. What happens when Jesus comes to live within us (see Colossians 1:13, NIV)?

_____

_____

33. After salvation, Satan's only hope of controlling us lies in what?

_____

_____

34. God will not deliver us from what?

_____

35. We must choose to stop our souls from doing what? How do we accomplish this?

_____

_____

_____

36. What statement of Paul's is this likened to in the text?

_____

_____

37. It is easier to resist and reject the pull of our old natures when we do what?

_____

_____

38. How do we accomplish this?

_____

_____

_____

_____

39. Even though we cannot loose the facts of our past experiences, we can loose what?

_____

_____

_____

40. This can only happen when you know how to do what?

_____

_____

_____

41. Why would you feel you had to constantly reinforce your own self-protective defenses?

_____

42. What does this put you under constant pressure to do?

_____
_____
_____
_____

43. What must you stop trusting in so you can rest in God's care?

_____

44. Complete a description of the three sources of the pain, need, and confusion in our unsurrendered souls.

Unmet needs:

_____
_____

Unhealed hurts:

_____
_____

Unresolved issues:

_____
_____

Unmet Needs

45. We try to do what about out unmet needs? God wants to do what?

_____
_____
_____
_____
_____

46. We are very fearful of admitting what about the world's "carrots"?

_____
_____

47. Our unmet needs are like what, doing what?

_____
_____
_____

48. How might a person accomplish killing off their unmet needs?

_____

49. What do coping mechanisms such as relationships, sex, alcohol, food, drugs do?

_____

50. When do they (the unmet needs) begin to prowl again?

_____

51. God will help us in this situation when we do what?

_____

Unmet Needs Produce Wrong Desires

52. Where do wrong desires come from?

_____

_____

53. What is behavior driven by unmet needs often seen as by others?

_____

_____

54. Give one example:

_____

_____

55. What might someone with a deep unmet need do to feel secure?

_____

56. What might someone with a deep unmet need do to feel accepted?

_____

_____

57. Someone with a deep unmet need to feel necessary might:

_____

_____

_____

58. What might be some consequences when we attempt to meet our own need?

_____

_____

59. How might those who are needy perceive themselves because of the reactions of others?

_____

_____

60. What must we learn that unmet needs are?

_____

61. In the hope of hiding these unmet needs, strongholds are erected. Why doesn't this resolve them?

_____

62. Wrong desires have the potential to become what?

_____
_____

63. Wrong desires bring about two other terrible situations. What are they?

_____
_____

Johnny-Be-Good and Johnny-Be-Bad Syndrome

64. What are wrong relationships almost always the result of?

_____

65. Explain the Johnny-Be-Good Syndrome:

_____
_____
_____
_____
_____

66. Explain the Johnny-Be-Bad Syndrome:

_____
_____
_____
_____
_____

67. What kind of relationships do unmet needs drive people into?

_____

Sacrificial Offerings to Unmet Needs

68. What is often used by Christians to pacify gnawing unmet needs?

_____

69. This substance abuse is often addressed at altar calls. **TRUE/FALSE**

> When God measures us, He puts the tape around our hearts, not our hips!

70. Rather than judging our weight, what is God waiting for?

_____

_____

71. What is far more effective than dealing with the symptoms and behaviors resulting from unmet needs?

_____

_____

72. We may be conscious of some of the things in our lives that make us eat wrongly. What are you aware of in your life if food is used to fulfill unmet needs?

_____

_____

_____

_____

73. What are four examples of the wrong reasons for eating?

_____

_____

_____

_____

_____

_____

_____

_____

74. There are other things our souls have buried beneath our level of consciousness. Our souls will not allow these things to be exposed willingly. Write down the three lines of the Food Addiction prayer that you feel are the most important to accomplishing this:

_____

_____

_____

_____

_____

Using Your Vulnerability Positively

75. When feeling vulnerable, what have many Christians learned to do?

_____

_____

_____

_____

_____

_____

_____

76. Do you have religious rituals? What might some of them be?

_____

_____

_____

_____

77. What is the good potential for vulnerability in your life?

_____

Unhealed Hurts

78. What causes unhealed hurts?

_____

79. What has the world taught us about our unhealed hurts?

_____

_____

_____

_____

80. What do our unhealed hurts telegraph?

_____

81. When we are hurting badly, what truth do we often want to ignore?

_____

_____

_____

82. When we are in constant pain from unhealed hurts, what do we often miss?

_____

_____

83. What do those who have deep unhealed hurts generally experience?

_____

_____

84. What does this create in our relationships with others?

_____

_____

85. What, again, is the threefold statement of purpose of the unsurrendered soul?

_____

86. True intimacy is always _____.

87. Forced intimacy is _____.

88. Many Christians equate intimacy with what?

_____

_____

Unhealed Hurts: Damaged Leaders

89. This wrong pattern of thinking is often used to justify doing what?

_____

_____

90. What will ultimately leak out of the ministry of someone who has buried issues?

_____

_____

91. Why is trying to self-contain these feeling never effective?

_____

_____

92. Satan cannot read your mind, but he can do what?

_____

_____

93. If he cannot get to your buried pain directly, what will he do?

_____

_____

_____

94. The most serious danger to your healing and spiritual growth does not come from Satan's plans against you—it comes from what?

_____

_____

95. How does Satan eventually get to your unhealed hurts?

_____

96. When is a minister always unable to minister wisely?

_____

_____

_____

97. It is never the right time to bring a corrective word when: (complete the statement)

_____

_____

98. Regardless of how much you want to help others, what can be a potential problem in your own soul?

_____

_____

_____

Unresolved Issues

99. When are unresolved issues birthed?

_____

_____

100. What do unresolved issues produce?

_____

_____

_____

101. What happened in the formative years of such an individual to create these wrong patterns of thinking?

_____

_____

_____

_____

102. What will this person try to do to create an intellectual and emotional structure where their soul feels safe?

_____

_____

_____

103. What gives this person cause for alarm?

_____

_____

104. What will the devil do to pressure the unresolved issues in our lives?

_____

_____

_____

105. If we react to these present-day replays instead of loosing the lies of their power to still control us, what can happen?

_____

_____

_____

> To be useful to God and others, we must get the layers off these no-trespassing zones of our souls. Until we do, God cannot heal us and we remain vulnerable to Satan's pressuring of our vulnerability. Our availability to God can be extremely hindered.

Unresolved Issues: Sources of Procrastination and Indecisiveness

106. Regardless of potential consequences, the procrastinator often chooses to do what?

_____

_____

107. When a child grows up in an environment where his or her choices frequently seem to cross unspoken, invisible boundaries producing negative consequences, what can happen?

_____

_____

108. To the procrastinator, avoided decisions are viewed as what?

_____

109. Rather than indecision, acts of procrastination are viewed as _____.

110. Some people choose to live their entire lives with procratination's lower-key stress rather than initiating what response?

_____

_____

111. The person who moves into an even deeper form of indecisiveness can see this "choice" as what?

_____

_____

112. This person chooses what over what?

_____

_____

_____

_____

Layers

113. What is the soul's bottom line defense system constructed from?

_____

_____

_____

114. The soul protects the core of it's power structure with layer upon layer of different self-protective, self-defensive mechanisms. What example is given of a similar type of strengthening by layering?

_____

_____

_____

115. Where does the layering occur?

_____

_____

116. These three areas are birthed by what?

_____

_____

117. What does the world teach we should do about this?

_____

_____

_____

_____

_____

_____

_____

118. Frightened, hopeless people buy into this because it provides an excuse for what?

_____

_____

_____

119. Why is it futile for us to work so hard to find others to blame for our current physical, mental, emotional, and spiritual states?

_____

120. If you insist upon clinging to all your soul's old "stuff," you can miss out on what?

_____

_____

121. You will always be motivated to do what?

_____

_____

_____

122. What will eventually happen to the things you have tried to hide in your soul?

_____

_____

_____

_____

Things to keep in mind as you continue through the rest of this workbook:

123. Strongholds keep:

_____

_____

124. Strongholds are the first level of defense against:

_____

_____

125. Layers keep:

_____

_____

126. What line of the soul's defense is this?

_____

_____

127. Binding and loosing prayers do what?

_____

_____

_____

_____

Special Note: There is a chart available to visually help you to understand the principles explained in these chapters.

Chapter 5 - Review

The most significant truths I found in this chapter are:

1. _____
   _____
   _____

2. _____
   _____
   _____

3. _____
   _____
   _____

4. _____
   _____
   _____

I applied these truths to my life as follows:

1. _____
   _____
   _____

2. _____
   _____
   _____

3. _____
   _____
   _____

4. _____
   _____

Chapter 5 - "Journey" Journal

Date: **Questions I have:**

Date: **Special insights I believe I have learned:**

Date: **Breakthroughs I have experienced:**

Chapter 5 - Prayer Journal

Date: **Prayer:**

Date: **Updates and special encouragements I've received from the Lord:**

Date: **Answers to prayers:**

6
Relationships and Agreements

1. What does the Holy Spirit often use to work out the impurities in our souls?

_____

2. When you have deep unmet needs in your life, you will generally be attracted to who?

_____

_____

3. This usually is a person with what?

_____

_____

> Beware of plunging into intense relationships with people who are eager to share their pain and "feel" yours.

4. What are these relationships full of?

_____

_____

5. Needy souls always seek ways to get what?

_____

_____

6. Why is it wise to be very prayerful in relating to counselors and leaders who identify with your problem and pain because of like experiences in their own lives?

_____

_____

_____

7. In their sincere desire to help, what might these "counselors" do?

_____

_____

8. Their advice can be colored by what, if they are not what, regardless of what?

_____

_____

_____

_____

9. You should avoid all people who are not yet whole. **TRUE/FALSE**

10. It is a lie that you don't dare miss what?

_____

_____

11. God can and will give wonderful relational experiences to you when?

_____

_____

Agenda of Love or Need?

12. What assumption are relationships usually formed around?

_____

_____

13. What should Christian relationships be based upon?

_____

_____

14. No matter how pure the human love coming out of a soul, it rarely has what?

_____

15. What causes your disappointment in others' reactions to your well-meant acts?

_____

_____

_____

16. God's divine agendas always cause us to seek what?

_____

_____

17. What enables us to do this?

_____

18. God's divine agenda working in us can be described as one that is what:

_____

_____

19. This love has no expectations and continues to what?

_____

_____

20. God's love helps _____ all _____ _____
and _____ _____ _____.

21. What are the worldly scenarios where games and agendas are often played out in a pursuit of socializing and companionship?

_____

_____

_____

22. Who generally suffers the most from these scenarios?

_____

_____

23. What is God always ready to give to us?

_____

24. What does natural man not understand about this?

_____

_____

25. Where does natural man continue to seek answers?

_____

26. Why do some people refuse to help others in any way?

_____

27. Other people cannot permanently fix our brokenness, nor can we permanently fix theirs. Where do we get permanently fixed?

_____

Releasing Your Imperfect People

28. We are not strong enough or smart enough to break what?

_____

_____

_____

29. What have we acquired from the actions of imperfect people?

_____

_____

30. What do we do when we don't know how to break the bondage cycle of the infectious imperfections of others?

_____

_____

_____

31. We need to stop blaming imperfect people, and stop rationalizing our reactive behaviors, and do what?

_____

_____

32. What affects us most in our lives? (circle one)
   a)   What others have done to us
   b)   What God has done for us

33. What are we called to be? (circle one)
   a)   Thermostats
   b)   Thermometers

34. What is the difference between thermostats and thermometers?
   a)_____
   b)_____

35. The burden of the baggage of imperfect people in your life affects you how?

_____

_____

_____

36. What are three main points regarding taking a stand against imperfect influences?

_____

_____

_____

_____

_____

_____

37. Can you purpose in your heart to use these principles and make them a reality? To make a memorial of your decision and a point of reference in the future, sign and date here if you have made that decision.

Signature: _____   Date: _____

Forgiveness Is the Catalyst of Miracles

38. Man's natural resources for extending grace and mercy are what?

_____

39. God will give you all grace and mercy to reach out and forgive others if what?

_____

_____

40. What creates clutter clogging up your capacity to receive forgiveness from God?

a)_____

b)_____

c)_____

d)_____

e)_____

41. What are these things, as referenced in 2 Corinthians 10:5 (KJV)?

_____

_____

> Second Corinthians 10:3-4 (AMP) tells us, "For the weapons of our warfare are not physical (weapons of flesh and blood), but they are mighty before God for the overthrow and destruction of strongholds."

42. How do you destroy the strongholds around and layers over your unforgiveness and pain?

_____

43. God's miraculous resources are only limited by what?

_____

_____

Making Room for Miracles

44. In the example given of 2 Kings 4:2-7, how did the woman set the limits of her own miracle?

_____

_____

45. Have you ever believed God for a miracle of restoration between you and another person, gone to them, and been rejected? What was the error factor you weren't aware of?

_____

_____

46. What should you have done instead?

_____

_____

47. Can you "float someone in a bucket"? **YES/NO**

48. What does that expression refer to?

_____

_____

_____

_____

49. What's the good news God is wanting you to understand?

_____

_____

Isn't There an Easier Way, God?

50. Faith comes by:

_____

51. Faith grows by:

_____

52. What will God do to make you grow if other less painful ways have not been fruitful?

_____

_____

53. The condition of your comfort zone is a good measuring device to register your faith level.
TRUE/FALSE

54. Good times and blessings do not produce what?

_____

_____

_____

55. Describe a soulish prayer:

_____

_____

56. In other words, "God, don't make me have to" what?

_____

_____

_____

The Power of Agreement

57. What does real unshakable faith require?

_____

58. The Greek words for "Abraham believed" in Galatians 3:6 (AMP) mean what?

_____

_____

59. Abraham's spirit's purpose was to do what?

_____

60. His soul's thoughts were to be what?

_____

61. His body's actions were to what?

_____

_____

62. To believe is more than what?

_____

63. God expects us to do what about our beliefs?

_____

_____

64. If we can't do what God expects us to do about our beliefs, what do we need to do?

_____

65. What is the example given to describe applying your belief system and testing its reality?

_____

_____

_____

_____

66. For a truthful response to the man's question, what had to change?

_____

_____

_____

_____

_____

67. How do you come into agreement within your own "troops"?

_____

_____

The Power in Wrong Agreement

68. What is the example given here about the power of wrong agreement, and what did God do to stop it?

_____

_____

_____

_____

_____

69. What did God say their agreement with each other meant?

_____

_____

70. What do wrong agreements produce?

_____

Agreeing with One Another

71. The Greek word translated as "gathered together" is *sunago* which comes from two other Greek words:
   a) *sun* means: _____

   b) *ago* means: _____

72. The "two or three" mentioned in Matthew 18:20 (who are "gathered together") have been what?

_____

_____

_____

_____

73. What happens when these kinds of agreements occur?

_____

_____

74. Praying with others who have come together by any influence other than the Holy Spirit can be what?

_____

_____

75. This sheds light on what?

_____

_____

76. What can you convince yourself of, when you are not led by the Holy Spirit?

_____

_____

77. When the Holy Spirit gathers people together to pray, what scriptural principle is enacted?

_____

_____

78. When you bind your will to God's will, what is released and why?

_____

_____

79. When you pray that way, what prayer are you in agreement with and why?

_____

_____

Praying in Unity

80. What is sometimes the only way for some Christians to come into one accord in prayer, and why?

_____

_____

81. When is it impossible to come into one accord with one another?

_____

_____

82. What can draw us into perfect unity?

_____

83. Binding ourselves to an awareness of Christ's blood and binding our minds to the mind of Christ has what effect on unity?

_____

_____

_____

_____

Agreeing with God

84. Where did God say He would "meet" with us?

_____

_____

85. Where is one place a stubborn, willful soul does not want to go?

_____

Missing the Meeting

86. What swings into action as soon as you try to seek to meet with God?

_____

_____

87. God will work _____ a surrendered soul.

88. But, God will actually _____ with a regenerated spirit.

89. Where does the spiritual blessing come from that your mind and emotions "feel" from the presence of God?

_____

God Will Not be Mocked

> Galatians 6:7 (AMP), "Do not be deceived and deluded and misled; God will not allow Himself to be sneered at—scorned, disdained or mocked (by mere pretentions or professions, or by His precepts being set aside)—he inevitably deludes himself who attempts to delude God. For whatever a man sows, that and that only is what he will reap.

90. In what three areas do we need to check ourselves as to whether or not we might be fooled about Galatians 6:7?

a)_____

b)_____

c)_____

91. Once the binding and loosing prayers have begun to work on dismantling the deception and denial of your soul, what comes next?

_____

_____

92. The author says something unfortunate occurred when she began to complain to others. What was it?

_____

_____

> Galatians 6:2-4 (AMP), "Bear (endure, carry) one another's burdens and troublesome moral faults, and in this way fulfill and observe perfectly the law of Christ, the Messiah, and complete what is lacking in your obedience to it. For if any person thinks himself to be somebody (too important to condescend to shoulder another's load), when he is nobody (of superiority except in his own estimation), he deceives and deludes and cheats himself. But let every person carefully scrutinize and examine and test his own conduct and his own work."

93. By resenting having to respond to so many people about the message God had blessed her with, the author says she "cursed herself" in two ways. What are they?

_____

_____

94. The author rationalized avoiding individual sharing. Name three rationalizations she made:

_____

_____

_____

_____

95. The author believes she would not have had many ensuing wonderful experiences if she had not recognized what?

_____

_____

_____

96. Obedience to God's _____ and _____ go hand-in-hand with the _____ He gives to you.

97. Reaping and sowing is a principle that applies to what?

_____

98. Whenever God gives you revelation, you need to what? Why?

_____

_____

99. God says to give (whatever!) and what will happen?

_____

_____

Chapter 6 - Review

The most significant truths I found in this chapter are:

1. _____
_____
_____

2. _____
_____
_____

3. _____
_____
_____

4. _____
_____
_____

I applied these truths to my life as follows:

1. _____
_____
_____

2. _____
_____
_____

3. _____
_____
_____

4. _____
_____
_____

Chapter 6 - "Journey" Journal

Date: **Questions I have:**

Date: **Special insights I believe I have learned:**

Date: **Breakthroughs I have experienced:**

Chapter 6 - Prayer Journal

Date: **Prayer:**

Date: **Updates and special encouragements I've received from the Lord:**

Date: **Answers to prayers:**

7
Soul Power and Soul-Ties

The spirit and the soul of man are totally different entities.

1. The spirit belongs to?

_____

2. The soul "belongs" to?

_____

3. The spirit is _____ conscious.

4. The soul is _____ conscious.

5. The body is _____ conscious.

6. Explain the "control tower" concept in this:

_____
_____
_____

7. What should not be choosing which world you will most identify with?

_____

8. The ability to organize and orchestrate the responsibility of the Garden of Eden was
_____ in Adam's _____.

9. Adam's astounding ability and power was like a _____ to
_____.

10. How does Satan initiate his works of darkness in the world?

_____

11. When Satan successfully tempts your soul into agreement with him, what will your body do?

_____
_____
_____

12. Sin is the natural outcome of what?

_____
_____

Where Did the Soul's Original Power Go?

13. The fall in the Garden produced what separation?

_____

14. What does the author believe God did to Adam's soul?

_____
_____

15. How does Watchman Nee describe what God did?

_____
_____

16. What does latent mean?

_____
_____

17. Man has not figured out what about his soul (for the most part)?

_____

18. What do many cults and "religions" exist to teach?

_____
_____

19. Some men and women have caused devastation and loss of lives through their soulish ability to control others. Name a few.

_____

20. Where soul power is concerned, what is Satan always ready to assist?

_____

21. Soul power released through man's own efforts will always be used for what?

_____

Why Hasn't God Done Something?

22. What is the general beginning of paranormal activities, such as psychics, divination, bending and moving of objects, mental telepathy, etc., and their general outcome?

_____

_____

_____

23. Why does the author believe God did not completely wipe out the power of the soul of man when he fell?

_____

_____

24. What is the author's view on the believers' souls' part in the outpouring of the latter days?

_____

_____

25. The "translators" or "interpreters" of this outpouring will be:

_____

_____

26. God's power will be manifested through _____ _____.

27. Supernatural power will pour into _____ _____ to be _____ in the natural through the _____ _____ and _____ of Christians here on Earth!

The Commission of the Human Soul

28. Unless our infinite human abilities are _____, _____, and _____, we will not be able to what?

_____

_____

29. What are our souls to become if they are surrendered to God?

_____

_____

30. In Daniel 11:32-33 (AMP), the people who know their God shall do what?

_____

_____

31. They who are wise and understand shall do what?

_____

32. Daniel 12:3-4, 10 (AMP), the teachers and those who are wise shall do what?

_____ ____

33. In Daniel 12:3-4, 10 (AMP), those who turn many to righteousness shall do what?

_____

34. In the same Daniel passage, what will happen to the wicked?

_____

_____

Many Seeking Soul Power

35. What are the groups, cultures, and "religions" doing to try to release the power within the soul of man?

_____

_____

_____

_____

36. What is the single governing principle here?

_____

_____

37. What does Revelation 18:13 say?

_____

_____

38. What truth have the Muslims found to be successful that few Christians act upon?

_____

_____

_____

The Christian's Deception

39. What must you know to "discern the truth"?

_____

40. How does the discerning or knowing come?

_____

_____

_____

_____

41. What will bring down many believers when things get really intense in these last days?

_____

_____

_____

42. Christians can faithfully do what four things and be lulled into complacency that all is well?

_____

_____

43. Describe the example given that shows the state of many Christians today?

_____

_____

_____

_____

_____

_____

The Mystery of Iniquity

44. Christians are adapting to what today?

_____

45. There is a gradual desensitization to what?

_____

46. In 2 Thessalonians 2:7 (KJV), who is "he who now letteth"?

_____

47. What is the usual belief regarding the "taking out of the way" passage of this verse?

_____

_____

_____

48. If the Holy Spirit was to be taken from the earth when the body of Christ was raptured, what would be undone?

_____

_____

_____

_____

49. What does the author say that the verse 2 Thessalonians 2:7 is telling us about the Holy Spirit and the Church?

_____

_____

_____

_____

50. What does the author say she needs to know and do regarding the tribulation?

_____

_____

_____

_____

Christian Soul Power is Going to be Exposed

51. Christians cannot function in soul power. **TRUE/FALSE**

52. What happens to soul power if two souls come into wrong agreement?

_____

53. If you are not aware of soul power from another person's soul what do you run the risk of?

_____

54. God's people are to be one _____ _____, but never one

_____ _____.

55. What is happening in many Christian meetings today concerning soul power?

_____

_____

_____

_____

56. Most of the ministers conducting these services believe what?

_____

_____

57. What are these ministers trying to do for God?

_____

_____

58. What are many of these ministers liable to experience in their lives?

_____

_____

> We must all learn to stop responding out of our souls to the gift-wrapping of the messengers and listen intently with our spirits to the message they are offering.

59. What are three questions we should ask ourselves in the months after we hear a minister's message?

_____

_____

_____

60. The author suggests "what" might happen if we knew too much about Christ's physical characteristics and mannerisms?

_____
_____

61. How should we receive every minister, leader, brother, and sister?

_____

Soul-Ties

62. We should not pray what kind of prayers?

_____
_____

63. When will we stop judging from our souls?

_____
_____

64. What are soulish prayers often like?

_____
_____

65. What can lead you into a soul tie with someone else?

_____
_____

66. Can you form a "soul-tie" with an evil spirit? How?

_____
_____
_____

67. Evil spirits do not have bodies, but they do they have what?

_____

68. What does Ezekiel 28 say about Lucifer's intelligence, determination, and pride?

_____
_____
_____
_____
_____
_____

69. The author recommends you stop doing what three things?
   a)_____
   b)_____
   c)_____

70. Soul-ties are often a factor when people can't get freedom from what?

_____

_____

David and Jonathan

71. First Samuel 18:1-3 (KJV) is the story of the meeting of David and Jonathan. Name one possible hidden agenda Jonathan might have had with regard to David?

_____

_____

_____

_____

72. Why is it not hard to believe Jonathan had such wrong motives?

_____

_____

73. First Samuel 19:1-3 tells about Saul wanting Jonathan to kill David. Why did David turn to his "soulmate," Jonathan, instead of to God?

_____

_____

74. Describe the souls of David and Jonathan.

_____

_____

_____

75. How did Saul's struggle with his soul affect his son Jonathan?

_____

_____

76. Why does the author say that Saul was doubleminded?

_____

_____

_____

77. First Samuel 20:4 (KJV), "Then said Jonathan unto David, Whatsoever thy soul desireth, I will even do it for thee." The Hebrew word used here for "soul" is *nephesh*. What does Gesenius say this particular use of *nephesh* means?

_____

_____

78. What is the point of this verse according to the author?

_____

_____

79. What was the condition of David's soul from the day he met Jonathan?

_____

80. What was the condition of David's soul before he met Jonathan?

_____

_____

_____

81. What happened to David, as he became increasing dependent upon the soulish resources of Jonathan?

_____

_____

82. What happened when the king's servants were about to identify David in Gath?

_____

_____

_____

83. Why did David fall so far spiritually when he was a "man after God's own heart"?

_____

_____

Jonathan's Soul

84. First Samuel 14 tells the story of Jonathan and Saul's hungry army. Saul swore his fighting men to obey what oath?

_____

_____

85. What did the hungry army find in the woods, and what did the soldiers do?

_____

_____

86. Had Jonathan heard the threat of the curse? What did he do?

_____

_____

87. The men told him about the curse. What was his response?

_____

_____

_____

_____

_____

_____

88. What was Jonathan expressing to the soldiers?

_____
_____
_____

89. Four chapters later in Chapter 18, David's peaceful, quiet soul came into agreement with this rebellious, disobedient, and disrespectful soul in Jonathan. What happened to David's soul?

_____
_____
_____
_____
_____

90. What continued to happen even after David turned his heart back to God?

_____
_____

No Such Thing as a Good Soul-Tie

91. What is a soul-tie?

_____

92. What do they appear to hold for each person involved?

_____

93. If one is seemingly forced or feels threatened into entering a wrong agreement, what is the "benefit" to them?

_____
_____

94. Several years earlier, the author entered into a wrong agreement with a Christian leader. What "benefit" did she think would come about?

_____
_____

95. After the Jezebel accusations in her early days of being a Christian, she did not know how to let go of what?

_____
_____

96. When identical circumstances resurfaced in the author's life at a later date, she had an instant fear of what?

_____
_____
_____

> Unresolved painful issues in our lives can cause us to repeat mistakes, or react in even worse ways when identical circumstances confront us again.

97. When difficult issues in your life are not resolved correctly the first time they come up, what does Satan do?

_____

_____

98. What are you liable to do?

_____

_____

> We should never attempt to deal with our unresolved issues by just trying to sweep them into that cavernous Christian cliché known as "under the blood." If a certain issue caused you great pain, confusion, and fear, only God's grace will allow that issue to be resolved and then placed "under the blood." The flaw in this "under the blood" Christian cliché is we cannot put things under the blood ourselves, especially when we do not know how to let go of them in the first place. Only the grace of God can heal and resolve all issues forever.

No Such Thing as No Choice

99. How do we often look at our tough choices?

_____

_____

_____

100. How does God look at our tough choices?

_____

_____

_____

> We always have a choice in every circumstance of our own lives.

101. A ninety-pound Christian woman being forced against the wall of a dark alley by a three hundred-pound man holding a knife to her throat has choices. What are two choices?
Choice #1:_____

_____

_____

Choice #2:_____

_____

_____

102. What is Choice #2 reflective of?

_____

_____

103. Why is there no fear in the regenerated spirit?

_____

_____

_____

104. By binding herself and the man to God's will, what has she relinquished?

_____

_____

_____

_____

Balance of Power in Soul-Ties

105. In a soul-tie, which soul is usually the stronger of the two?

_____

106. The word "stronger" is not descriptive of force, but of what?

_____

_____

107. Where might this source come from?

_____

_____

_____

_____

_____

108. What is the example given here of a dominant soul and its control?

_____

_____

_____

109. What is the general soul condition of women who use soul power to control?

_____

110. Women are very capable of affecting what? By what means?

_____

_____

_____

_____

111. Co-dependency is a term that has been overused, but is very descriptive. How was that term originally used?

_____

_____

_____

112. Both persons in soulish relationships are seeking to get something, regardless of what?

_____

_____

113. The neediest soul in these relationships often accepts what, and why?

_____

_____

The Soul and Grief

114. Where is grief experienced?

_____

115. What can prolong the period of grieving for someone who has lost a loved one?

_____

_____

116. Does this mean we should deny remaining feelings about one who has been lost?

_____

_____

117. Residual soul-ties can be severed if what?

_____

_____

118. Why would the one grieving not want to sever them?

_____

_____

119. How can those in extended grieving begin to see themselves?

_____

_____

120. What did David do when his son was so ill? List four things:

_____

_____

_____

_____

121. What were David's words to his servants after he released his grief to God?

_____

_____

_____

122. When God does not give us the answer we want, what may be happening?

_____

_____

_____

Grieving Over Other Losses

123. What else might we grieve over?

_____

_____

124. What prophet experienced grief over unfulfilled expectations? What did the prophet do? What did God tell him?

_____

_____

_____

_____

_____

125. How has the author paraphrased God's answer to Samuel?

_____

_____

126. What can happen when your soul will not let go of something God has rejected?

_____

_____

_____

127. Some people will wear themselves out trying to make something work that God has rejected. What should they do?

_____

_____

_____

_____

_____

128. What might God's instructions be?

_____

_____

Soul-Ties Between Man and Wife

129. Where must the love in a perfect union in marriage come from?

_____

130. What love never grows bored or disappointed or cold when time passes and circumstances change? Why not?

_____

_____

_____

_____

131. When does the soul-tie between husband and wife establish itself?

_____

_____

_____

132. What do these soul-ties cause in a marriage?

_____

_____

_____

133. What happens when one partner's dependency upon the other is excessively out of balance? Initially and eventually?

_____

_____

_____

_____

134. Where do the terms "I don't love you anymore" or "I can't stand you anymore, and I want you out of my life" come from?

_____

_____

_____

_____

Because of your new knowledge about soul-ties, did you see yourself in any of these pages as being in wrong agreements with others? If you do and you want to change, use this as an opportunity to place another memorial here to the Lord for a change in your life. Choose now to loose all soul-ties you have entered into—even if it will disturb some of your relationships. Relationships that are seemingly at rest until you pray and use the key of loosing to sever and cut them apart have unhealthy elements in them. The breaking of the existing soul-ties will allow God to work in these relationships. This loosing and breaking is done by prayer, not by verbal confrontation.

Signature: _____ Date: _____

Chapter 7 - Review

The most significant truths I found in this chapter are:

1. _____
_____
_____

2. _____
_____
_____

3. _____
_____
_____

4. _____
_____
_____

I applied these truths to my life as follows:

1. _____
_____
_____

2. _____
_____
_____

3. _____
_____
_____

4. _____
_____
_____

Chapter 7 - "Journey" Journal

Date: **Questions I have:**

Date: **Special insights I believe I have learned:**

Date: **Breakthroughs I have experienced:**

Chapter 7 - Prayer Journal

Date: **Prayer:**

Date: **Updates and special encouragements I've received from the Lord:**

Date: **Answers to prayers:**

8
Now, Just Do It!

1. John 14:12 (NIV) tells us that Jesus said, "I tell you the truth, _____ who has _____ _____ _____ will do what I _____ _____ _____. He will do _____ _____ _____ than these, because I am going to the Father."

> Christians are meant to be walking on water, stilling storms, raising the dead, opening blind eyes, and more!

2. According to Thayer, the word "faith" used in this passage means:

_____

_____

3. This kind of faith serves Christ how?

_____

4. What did Jesus give us the keys to the Kingdom for?

_____

_____

_____

_____

5. What is our job?

_____

_____

_____

Spiritual Reality or Soulish Role-Playing

6. Write out Ephesians 4:22-24 (AMP) here (as in the book) and then circle what you believe to be the most important points.

_____

_____

_____

_____

_____

_____

_____

_____

7. What do we do when we don't know how to strip off and discard our old natures?

_____

_____

8. What is a genuine fresh mental and spiritual attitude?

_____

_____

9. We will never integrate what?

_____

_____

Let's Get It Right

10. God doesn't believe in wasting what?

_____

> "Are you kidding? I'm not spending eternity with you the way you are now!"

11. Everything you've been through can be turned into what?

_____

_____

12. Our souls have no _____ - _____ _____,
and they _____ _____.

13. What has to happen before you will ever force your soul to change?

First: _____

_____

_____

Second: _____

_____

_____

Third: _____

_____

_____

14. If you really want to change, what is one of the first things you should do?

_____

Reality Checks On Your Prayers

15. How should you pray for those who have used and abused you?

_____

_____

_____

16. How should you pray for your straying children and family members?

_____

_____

_____

17. How should you pray for spiteful, backstabbing co-workers?

_____

_____

_____

18. How should you pray for your pastor who you think isn't dynamic enough?

_____

_____

_____

_____

19. How should you pray for the one chosen to fill the church position you wanted?

_____

_____

_____

_____

20. We will get into God's will faster when we stop doing what four things?

_____

_____

_____

_____

_____

21. What do we know and understand as if looking through a glass darkly?

_____

_____

22. We do not understand His ways of what?

_____

_____

23. We get all caught up in what?

_____

_____

_____

24. When this happens, God is probably doing what?

_____

_____

The Shortest Distance to Victory

25. Where does the shortest distance between the two points of frustration and freedom go?

_____

26. Where does the shortest distance between the two points of anger and peace go?

_____

27. Where does the shortest distance between the two points of self-vengeance and forgiveness go?

_____

28. What questions should we ask ourselves when something bothers us?
    a)_____

    _____

    b)_____

    _____

    c)_____

    _____

29. Where should we focus when a "barb" is sent our way?

_____

30. If we uncover a hot spot in our soul, how should we pray?

_____

_____

_____

31. What does Galatians 5:2 say, in your own words?

_____

_____

Stop Pretending Everything is Just Fine

32. Galatians 6:7 speaks of pretending and professing something that isn't. In what three ways do we do this?

*First:*_____

_____

*Second:*_____

_____

*Third:*_____

_____

33. Are any of these pretensions or professions acceptable to God? **YES/NO**

34. You spiritually fulfill God's precepts and principles by focusing your belief in three ways. Already having done whatever practical things you know to do such as praying, avoiding known temptations, and reading God's Word, what are the three ways?

*Spirit:*_____

_____

_____

_____

*Soul:*_____

_____

_____

_____

*Body:*_____

_____

_____

_____

35. What does the word "synergy" mean?

_____

_____

_____

36. What is the key word in the successful synergism of your life?

_____

37. It is not helpful to your spirit's efforts to lift you up when you are affected by your own soulish and fleshly reactions. Give some examples of these reactions:

Mind is _____

Mouth is_____

Lower lip is_____

Face is _____

Eyes are _____

Knees are _____

Hands are _____

38. When your soul is fearful or unhappy, what will it do?

_____

_____

_____

39. What is the first step to avoiding this trap?

_____

40. What is a good description of the believer's soul, spirit, and body being in alignment with His plans and purposes?

_____

_____

God Wouldn't—Would He?

41. How did the author rationalize and justify the way she was praying for her neighbors?

_____

_____

42. Do you remember what a personal stronghold is?

_____

_____

43. After 18 months of logical prayers, what did the author finally figure out?

_____

_____

44. How did she change her prayers for her loud neighbors?

_____

_____

_____

_____

45. What did she hope their next neighbors did?

_____

_____

Praying Right Prayers

46. What complaint is frequently heard from Christians working in secular jobs?

_____

_____

_____

> If all the Christians in the Body of Christ only worked at home or with other Christians, who would witness to the non-Christian worker? Who would pray for them when they lost a loved one or received a bad report from a doctor? Who would they turn to when they needed hope and solutions to hard things they were having to walk through? Who would show them that Jesus loved them even in the midst of their bad language and dirty jokes?

47. Who can push Christians to grow beyond their comfort zones?

_____

48. Who best exposes self-righteous Christians' lack of love, convicting them to change?

_____

49. What could a non-believer be thinking regarding the believer, even though he or she might not say it aloud?

_____

_____

_____

_____

_____

_____

_____

_____

50. Non-believers recognize when believers are wanting to do what?

_____

51. A _____ and true, _____ and available _____ of God would _____ _____ _____ starving in a _____ while he went off to _____ at the Father's _____!

52. When people don't like a Christian in the workplace, what might be the problem?

_____

_____

53. Jesus did what six things with betrayers, thieves, whores, unbelievers, tax collectors, street beggars, and others that so many of us find hard to love?

_____

_____

_____

> If God is not able to change us enough to love hard-to-love people regardless of their rough edges, then how can they ever believe He can change them?

54. The carnal mind and the closed spirit of the unbeliever cannot receive what?

_____

55. What can a carnal mind that is in pain or frozen by fear recognize?

_____

_____

56. When God places believers in certain jobs, what can we call these jobs?

_____

57. If a Christian cannot verbally speak of the issues of the Gospel, what can they do?

_____

_____

58. What is the believer's real job?

_____

59. What is the believer's cover?

_____

A Very "Now" Gospel

60. What is the beauty of the good news of the Gospel of Jesus Christ?

_____

_____

61. Where does Jesus meet us?

_____

_____

> Jesus meets us in the middle of all the things we have done that have caused other people pain, and all He says is this: "Are you ready to let me begin the untangling and fixing of all of this?"

62. The author was saved during a time of spiritual teaching that said what?

_____

_____

63. She was quite surprised to realize that we're probably _____ _____ on God's _____ of _____ to bring a _____.

At Least God Showed Them Grace

64. When you do not know how to pray effectively for your childrens' freedom from mistakes that you made while raising them, they are set up to what?

_____

_____

65. There is nothing you can do to erase what?

_____

_____

66. When family members, who are focused on guarding their pain, are put together under one roof, what negative things can happen?

_____

_____

_____

67. Those full of pain and fear will do what?

_____

_____

68. You cannot loose the mistakes you have made, but you can loose what?

_____

_____

69. Write here the sentence that touches you the most in the Family Members Prayer:

_____

_____

_____

Loosing Grave Clothes from Others

70. What untruth has the Body of Christ been taught for years?
*You can't help someone who*_____
*You can't heal someone who*_____
*You can't save someone who*_____
*You can't deliver someone who*_____

71. What is the spiritual parallel of loosing negative things from another person?
_____
_____

72. From the account on page 190 and 191 of *Breaking the Power* tell the significant aspects of this story in your own words.
_____
_____
_____
_____
_____
_____

73. Who did Jesus tell to remove the grave clothes from Lazarus?
_____

74. What are the grave clothes we are to loose from those who are bound up today?
_____
_____

75. What might some of those hindrances be?
_____
_____

76. Your loved ones have heard His voice. What is it they do not understand?
_____
_____

77. Where do most of the grave clothes come from?
_____
_____

78. What is another source of grave clothes?
_____
_____
_____
_____

79. How have we done a great deal of harm in trying to get others to agree in prayer?

_____

_____

80. What is one of the most incredible aspects of praying the binding and loosing prayers? You do not:

_____

_____

_____

_____

81. And you do not have to:

_____

_____

_____

82. How do you then pray for those bound in grave clothes and darkness?
You bind: _____

_____

_____

You loose: _____

_____

_____

83. What is the Holy Spirit's job that you can stop trying to do?

_____

84. When are the grave clothes hung?

_____

_____

_____

85. What happens to these details when they are spoken into existence?

_____

86. As a result, what can happen when prayers are answered for salvation and restoration to the family of God, and the lost sheep return to the fold?

_____

_____

87. In struggling with their unsurrendered souls, the devil, and feelings of shame and guilt, what else must they overcome as well?

_____

_____

_____

What Right Do We Have to Bind Others in Prayer Anyway?

88. What gives us the right to bind another person's will to God's will? Or another person's mind to the mind of Christ?

Proverbs 24:11-12, KJV: _____

_____

_____

_____

_____

Proverbs 24:11-12, AMP: _____

_____

_____

_____

_____

_____

_____

Proverbs 24:11-12, NIV: _____

_____

_____

_____

_____

Proverbs 24:11-12, The Message: _____

_____

_____

_____

Jude 23, KJV: _____

Jude 23, AMP: _____

Jude 23, NIV: _____

Jude 23, The Message: _____

_____

89. These verses are not speaking of whom?

_____

_____

90. Those who stand at the edge of Satan's flames stand there as a result of what?

_____

_____

91. What does someone at the edge of hell's flame need?

_____

92. What might a passive protest or gentle testimony be at this moment?

_____

_____

93. What holds some of us back from confronting someone's spiritual state?

_____

_____

_____

94. How can you break through your shyness and/or pride, to help those facing the flames of hell?

_____

95. In God's eyes, when are you most righteously aggressive and spiritually tall?

_____

_____

> What excuse will we have to offer God when He asks, "What did you do to prevent that lamb's death sentence?"

96. Write here the one sentence you feel is most powerful in the Backslidden and Unsaved Prayer:

_____

_____

_____

Chapter 8 - Review

The most significant truths I found in this chapter are:

1. _____
_____
_____

2. _____
_____
_____

3. _____
_____
_____

4. _____
_____
_____

I applied these truths to my life as follows:

1. _____
_____
_____

2. _____
_____
_____

3. _____
_____
_____

4. _____
_____
_____

Chapter 8 - "Journey" Journal

Date: **Questions I have:**

Date: **Special insights I believe I have learned:**

Date: **Breakthroughs I have experienced:**

Chapter 8 - Prayer Journal

Date: **Prayer:**

Date: **Updates and special encouragements I've received from the Lord:**

Date: **Answers to prayers:**

9
Tying Up Loose Ends

1. What is taught to many in the church regarding out of control emotions such as anger or rage?

_____

_____

2. What is often the actual problem when these emotions erupt?

_____

_____

_____

3. When buried anger is never resolved, what happens to it?

_____

_____

_____

4. Our souls store up raging feelings about injustices done to us, sometimes for years. Why?

_____

_____

5. When you are deceptively lulled into believing you have won a battle, Satan and your soul manage to keep you in what state?

_____

_____

6. What is the real problem?

_____

7. What happens when the disappearance of symptoms causes you to believe whatever charade the devil and/or your soul happens to be currently running on you?

_____

8. Satan is aware of every player in a charade, but what does your soul generally think?

_____

Binding and Loosing Naturally

9. After doing a back flip, what did the author bind and loose?

_____

_____

_____

_____

10. When does real victory come?

_____

_____

Doing What God Has Said to Do

11. God gives opportunities to us in prayer and ministry to find out what about ourselves?

_____

12. How can we be influenced in the natural as we are praying for others?

_____

_____

_____

_____

13. What must we stop depending upon in order to pray correctly for others?

_____

14. We need to minister in what way to minister according to God's leading only?

_____

_____

_____

15. Don't ever get to the point where you think you don't need what?

_____

_____

16. What is the admonishment on page 204 of *Breaking the Power* regarding one of God's lambs?

_____

_____

_____

_____

17. Who is the only one who wins in this case?

_____

Attitudes of the Unsurrendered Soul

18. The church world's emphasis on spiritual warring against Satan should be replaced with more emphasis on what?

_____

19. Second Timothy 2:1-3, 7-9 of *The Message* reads, "The first thing I want you to do is pray. Pray every way you know how, for everyone you know. Pray especially for rulers and their governments to rule well so we can be quietly about our business of living simply, in humble contemplation. This is the way our Savior God wants us to live . . . ." (complete the Scripture):

_____
_____
_____
_____
_____

20. What is much of the current spiritual warfare today?

_____
_____

21. Satan may be stopped from crossing the "blood line," but rebellious attitudes of our unsurrendered souls are what?

_____

22. Name six examples of rebellious attitudes of the soul:

_____
_____
_____

23. Unforgiveness is not what?

_____
_____
_____

24. Unforgiveness is what?

_____
_____

25. What does an outward expression of an attitude of the unsurrendered soul always produce?

_____

26. Explain the example of unforgiveness in Matthew 18:23 in your own words:

_____

_____

_____

_____

_____

27. Tormentors as used in verse 34 of Matthew 18 (KJV) means what?

_____

_____

_____

_____

_____

28. These definitions perfectly describe what?

_____

29. When the attitude of unforgiveness is not addressed and resolved by a believer, there is no what?

_____

_____

_____

_____

30. It is easier to impart forgiveness to what person?

_____

_____

31. Rationalizing and holding onto unforgiveness after the "sun goes down" results in what?

_____

_____

_____

32. What would our souls rather do than forgive someone we have decided does not deserve our forgiveness?

_____

Spiritual Survival Modes

33. We can apply the keys of the Kingdom to what "limitations"?

_____

34. Why is it ineffective to bind evil spirits?

_____

_____

_____

35. The devil will let you win what?

_____

_____

_____

36. We are spending too much time today in spiritual warfare with our supposed external enemy and too little time doing what?

_____

_____

37. The real spiritual battle should be fought against:

_____

_____

38. The strongholds we build within our carnal natures cause what to happen?

_____

_____

_____

39. Who are the only believers who truly frighten our external "already defeated" enemy?

_____

40. When it is time to move out for God, what is a hard position to have to come back from?

_____

41. There is little room for God in what equation?

_____

_____

42. There is no _____ _____ to hide _____
a _____ when you're six feet tall!

No Fear?

43. There is an intense kind of fear that can cause you to freeze up, give up, even throw up. How do non-believers deal with many of these fears?

_____

_____

_____

44. What might they do to "laugh" at fear?

_____

45. What is the basic problem with these kinds of "no fear" drills?

_____

_____

46. When they read these horror books and see these horror movies, what happens?

_____

Dismantling Fear

47. Where can fear come from?

_____
_____
_____
_____

48. How have many of us tried to create certain environments in which we feel relatively safe from fear?

_____
_____
_____
_____

49. How do we try to control a lot of our fear?

_____
_____
_____

50. Intense self-control can be convincing as long as what?

_____
_____

51. Describe someone who really has the peace of God.

_____

52. A soul-enforced "peace zone" can resist anything if a person's will is strong enough. **TRUE/FALSE**

53. What can dissolve all fear?

_____
_____
_____

54. Write out one sentence you feel encouraged by in the Breaking Fear Prayer:

_____
_____
_____

Faithless Fleeces

55. The author refused to let up on prayers that her soul was praying because she was afraid God would think what?

_____

_____

_____

56. She sometimes thinks God kept her around just for what?

_____

_____

57. God usually ignores what?

_____

58. Who does not ignore soulish prayers?

_____

59. Satan is quite capable of answering soulish prayers as well as what?

_____

_____

60. If you've prayed and prayed and have not received an answer from God, what have you probably done?

_____

_____

_____

61. If you have prayed amiss and you are convinced you know what the answer should be, and you won't open up a surrendered line to hear God, what may you resort to?

_____

_____

62. What is this gambit?

_____

_____

63. Where do fleeces usually originate?

_____

64. Who will drop fake fleeces in front of you?

_____

65. It is not hard to believe whatever you want to believe when:

_____

Taking a Walk with God

66. What should you do if you do not seem to hear anything on a given issue that is not turning out the way you think it should?

_____

_____

_____

67. God's divine communications work best when you do what?

_____

_____

68. What has caused many in the Body of Christ to land in all kinds of situations that abound with sticky tentacles and prickly ropes of bondage known as consequences?

_____

_____

69. Loosing the natural consequences of a disobedient act **WILL/WILL NOT** make them go away. (circle one)

70. Why might you have to go through the "school of consequences"?

_____

_____

_____

71. What can be deactivated by loosing prayers?

_____

_____

_____

_____

72. Binding yourself to God's timing does not give you license to be impetuous or lazy. Why not?

_____

_____

_____

73. What could be the hindrance to the answer that you think is best?

_____

_____

74. What would happen if we were left to our own paths?

_____

_____

_____

_____

75. God responds quickly to the right prayers of believers who are what?

_____

76. No matter what happens between the prayer and the answer, what is God doing?

_____

Desperately Waiting for God

77. What must you do when you are desperately, frantically waiting on God for an answer?

_____

_____

78. Why is God so calm about some of our frantic situations?

_____

_____

_____

79. How does He look at things?

_____

80. What does binding ourselves to God's timing do?

_____

_____

81. What should you do while waiting for God to answer?

_____

_____

82. Why do we have most of the New Testament today?

_____

_____

83. Paul _____ and _____. Good plan!

84. When you are in conflict about whether or not God really knows what you need the most, what must you recognize?

_____

_____

85. Who should be in charge of your belief system? Why?

_____

_____

86. What will never be equally yoked in right beliefs?

_____

87. Our conscious awareness of what we really believe resides where?

_____

88. How do the following types of people react or respond to the concept of God being in control?

Non-believers:

_____

_____

_____

Double-minded believers:

_____

_____

_____

_____

_____

Spiritually-free believers:

_____

_____

_____

_____

89. Don't tell God you can't wait for Him to bring you to what?

_____

_____

Chapter 9 - Review

The most significant truths I found in this chapter are:

1. _____
_____
_____

2. _____
_____
_____

3. _____
_____
_____

4. _____
_____
_____

I applied these truths to my life as follows:

1. _____
_____
_____

2. _____
_____
_____

3. _____
_____
_____

4. _____
_____
_____

Chapter 9 - "Journey" Journal

Date: **Questions I have:**

Date: **Special insights I believe I have learned:**

Date: **Breakthroughs I have experienced:**

Chapter 9 - Prayer Journal

Date: **Prayer:**

Date: **Updates and special encouragements I've received from the Lord:**

Date: **Answers to prayers:**

10
Are You Ready for Your Future?

1. God will use every believer who is diligently trying to do what?

_____

_____

2. What four things do not matter to God when He sees you working to overcome your soul's control?

_____

_____

_____

3. When you finally make a unified body, soul, and spirit, "no-holds-barred-burn-the-bridges-go-all-out-for-it" decision for God, what will He do?

_____

_____

_____

_____

4. If you have not known how to step into walking in God's path of purpose for your life where He empowers you and supplies everything you need to fulfill His directives, what have you missed?

_____

> You now have the understanding you need to strip away all the layers of camouflage that have been hiding the doorway from you.

We Will Impact Nations

5. We have been too busy doing what to pray as much as we should for our leaders?

_____

_____

6. We can only banish darkness by doing what?

_____

7. What do you bind and loose in praying in agreement with others for leaders?

_____

_____

_____

_____

8. You should especially loose what?

_____

9. Speaking spiritual slander regarding our leaders and our country is easy when:

_____

_____

10. What do the Scriptures say about the authority over us?

_____

_____

11. What can we blame, at least in part, for the judgmental and critical decline of Christian attitudes toward our leaders today?

_____

_____

_____

12. Write out 2 Chronicles 7:14, KJV:

_____

_____

_____

_____

_____

_____

13. Whose responsibility is it to change this nation?

_____

14. Who has failed the hurting and dying of this nation?

_____

How Should We Pray for Our Leaders?

15. Pray that out leaders will receive what two things?

_____

_____

Read the Breaking the Power Prayer for Government Leaders and purpose in your heart to remember our leaders with prayer. If you will do this, sign here as another memorial of meeting with the Lord in agreement with His Holy Word.

Signature: _____ Date: _____

Today's Church Leaders

16. We cannot minister beyond what?

_____
_____

17. The heart cannot be taught or trained beyond what point?

_____

18. What will settle the sheep in these final days?

_____
_____
_____
_____
_____
_____

19. We may have to do what to receive God's anointing?

_____
_____
_____

20. If we have to invest that much time to get the anointing past our flesh every time God gives us a sacred appointment, what is happening?

_____
_____

21. We need to make room for what within ourselves?

_____
_____

22. How must we progress through the stages of our maturity?

_____

We need to loose all of the preconceived ideas and wrong beliefs we may have ever formed about how we can anticipate God's will and His ways of doing things in these last days. This needs to be accomplished for Him to speak important facets of His deeper truths to us and for us to pray clearly and purely to Him.

Twelve-Step Program for a Progressive Prayer Life

23. What is the "guaranteed program/methodology/formula for a progressive prayer life that will not fail!"? Write it down and make sure you don't lose it.

Step 1:_____

Step 2:_____

Step 3:_____

Step 4:_____

Repeat what?_____

24. What's the fastest way to get out of a locked brick building?

_____

25. What is the beauty of the promise of Matthew 16:19?

_____

_____

_____

_____

Cooperating With God's Will for Others

26. Where does the challenge frequently come from when the author speaks on our right to pray binding and loosing prayers for other people?

_____

27. What is her explanation for that? What can their intense concern cause?

_____

_____

_____

_____

28. What is the translation of Matthew 16:19 by Dr. Alfred Marshall's KJV-NIV Interlinear Bible telling the Body of Christ?

_____

_____

_____

_____

_____

> Is it not mind-boggling that God, for some infinitely incredible reason, wants His people to be a key part of the earthly manifestation of things already settled in heaven?

29. Write author's restatement of JB Phillips words about any wrong outcome from prayers using the keys of the Kingdom:

_____
_____
_____
_____
_____
_____

30. All prayers from hungry hearts are heard by God, but some are more what than others?

_____
_____

"Letting Go and Letting God" Be God

31. God wants to involve us in a manifestation of His will here on earth, particularly with what group of people?

_____
_____

32. When we're filled with fear, insecurity, and touchiness, what will we most likely do when God presses us beyond familiar ground?

_____

33. What hinders us from fulfilling the really big assignments He is waiting to give us?

_____
_____

34. God cannot heal our wounds until we do what?

_____
_____

35. Lion-hearted believers do not always have an edge in what?

_____

36. When will cooperating with God's final healing processes be the easiest?

_____
_____

37. What will open up the floodgates of God's supernatural, miracle-working power?

_____
_____
_____
_____

38. Everyone who holds an end-time position in God's army must learn how to do what?

_____

_____

_____

39. Who are these people?

_____

40. What must we all be willing to do at this point in history?

_____

_____

_____

41. What dimension will God attempt to move us all into?

_____

_____

_____

_____

_____

42. Every Christian's expectations of these final last days is too finite. Who will "the call to come" be extended to?

_____

_____

_____

43. What is the only prerequisite to this call?

_____

_____

44. God is holding out His hand to lead His people where?

_____

The Anniversary Party

45. List at least four things God said about the people who had been at the party:

_____

_____

_____

_____

_____

_____

_____

_____

46. Those who recognized how different the author was were astounded—not at her—but at who?

_____

_____

Reaching the Unreachable

47. What is the only thing that is going to change this last generation?

_____

_____

48. Too many Christians invalidate their "wonderful" testimonies by doing what on a daily basis?

_____

_____

_____

49. The world watches and wonders why:

_____

_____

_____

_____

_____

_____

50. People everywhere are still waiting to know a supernatural God. Why?

_____

_____

51. We still often stumble through hard spots. Why?

_____

_____

_____

52. What is your favorite part of Ephesians 2:10 (AMP)?

_____

_____

Givers of Grace

53. What three things does the author think God will ask His children when they get to heaven?

_____

_____

_____

_____

_____

54. It is hard to extend grace to who?

_____

_____

55. We must stop deciding what about dispensing grace?

_____

_____

56. God saw something in the author's heart during all of her scuffles with Him that told Him what?

_____

_____

_____

_____

_____

_____

Reality-Checks For a Servant's Heart

57. What is one of the author's reality checks?

_____

_____

58. What does your soul's "Oscar-potential" mean, according to the author?

_____

59. When the author runs a reality check on her soul, what does her soul usually do?

_____

_____

_____

60. Why is that a big mistake on her soul's part?

_____

_____

_____

61. Whenever the author failed a reality check and ran her mini-resume, what did she always end up wishing?

_____

_____

62. What does the author say she would have done and said to the pastor (calling from another city) ten years earlier?

_____

_____

_____

_____

63. What would this have created?

_____

_____

64. What would the pastor have been convinced about?

_____

_____

65. What did the author learn from driving the woman pastor's car and doing what she asked?

_____

_____

_____

_____

_____

Pull the Plug on Your Pride

66. What should you do if you lack a servant's attitude?

_____

_____

_____

_____

_____

_____

67. What will effectively take your unmet needs out of the realm of your soul's manipulation?

_____

68. As long as your soul can manipulate your unmet need, it can do what else?

_____

_____

_____

69. You can't just act humble when you know you're being watched. **TRUE/FALSE**

70. If your humility is fake, God will eventually do what?

_____

71. God will also expose what when you try to meet your own needs?

_____

72. The author says she is motivated to be constantly loosing layers. Why?

_____

_____

_____

True Humility

73. Who was the man who impressed the author with his true humility?

_____

74. What does the author say she will never forget about this world-famous, mighty man of God? Why?

_____
_____
_____
_____
_____
_____

75. Have you met anyone in your life like that? How did that affect your life?

_____
_____
_____
_____
_____

We've reached the end of _Breaking the Power_, but you have just begun a freedom voyage in a destiny revelation for your life and the lives of your loved ones.

Bon Voyage!

Chapter 10 - Review

The most significant truths I found in this chapter are:

1. _____
   _____
   _____

2. _____
   _____
   _____

3. _____
   _____
   _____

4. _____
   _____
   _____

I applied these truths to my life as follows:

1. _____
   _____
   _____

2. _____
   _____
   _____

3. _____
   _____
   _____

4. _____
   _____
   _____

Chapter 10 - "Journey" Journal

Date: **Questions I have:**

Date: **Special insights I believe I have learned:**

Date: **Breakthroughs I have experienced:**

Chapter 10 - Prayer Journal

Date: **Prayer:**

Date: **Updates and special encouragements I've received from the Lord:**

Date: **Answers to prayers:**

612-XI